# Cutting Edge Sales

# Cutting Edge Sales

Confessions of Success, Influence & Self-Fulfillment
From The World's Finest Knife Dealers

**Jon Berghoff**

Foreword by Jeffrey Gitomer

Stories and Secrets from:
Jon Berghoff, Dan Casetta, Carl Drew, Brad Britton, John Ruhlin, Jon
Vroman, Fi Mazanke, Ranjeet Pawar, Jerry Liu, John Edwin, Paulette
Tucciarone, John Israel, Adam Stock, Jason Scheckner, Hal Elrod

New York

# Cutting Edge Sales
## Confessions of Success, Influence & Self-Fulfillment
### From the World's Finest Knife Dealers

CUTCO is a registered trademark of Cutco Corporation, New York

ISBN 978-1-60037-623-8

Library of Congress Control Number: 2009924958

# MORGAN · JAMES
### THE ENTREPRENEURIAL PUBLISHER

Morgan James Publishing, LLC
1225 Franklin Ave., STE 325
Garden City, NY 11530-1693
Toll Free 800-485-4943
www.MorganJamesPublishing.com

In an effort to support local communities, raise awareness and funds, Morgan James Publishing donates one percent of all book sales for the life of each book to Habitat for Humanity. Get involved today, visit **www.HelpHabitatForHumanity.org**.

# Praise for Jon Berghoff and *Cutting Edge Sales*

"Look at what Jon Berghoff has done here. This is magnificent. Your sales will explode. The sales world will change because of *Cutting Edge Sales.*"

**Ivan R. Misner, Ph.D., Founder of BNI and *NY Times* Bestselling Author of *Masters of Sales***

"I started in direct sales: nothing taught me more about the sales process and the importance of continuous learning than that experience. Everybody needs the practical wisdom contained in *Cutting Edge Sales*: it is a historic, revolutionary memoir!"

**Brian Tracy, Chairman and CEO Brian Tracy International, Bestselling Author of over 45 books, including *21 Success Secrets of Self Made Millionaires***

"Outstanding! I've seen many authors and business owners look for ways to give back, but *Cutting Edge Sales* is truly one of a kind. Your business will transform – as will many lives across borders you may never see – because of this philanthropic book."

**Jay Conrad Levinson, Author of the *"Guerrilla Marketing"* Book Series**

"It is rare that a book has this kind of power - before even being opened – because of what it represents. When you buy this book, others will achieve their dreams. When you read this book, you will achieve yours!"

**Matthew Kelly, Founder and President, Floyd Consulting, Bestselling Author of *The Rhythm of Life* and *The Dream Manager***

"*Cutting Edge Sales* is guaranteed to send positive Ripples across the market place, and across the globe, in a way that is rarely achieved with just one book!"

**Steve Harper, Author of the Bestselling Book, *The Ripple Effect***

"Jon knows what it takes to create instant influence with anyone. More importantly, he knows how to teach YOU how to replicate the same sales results. My organization's sales went through the roof when Jon came into my life, and I'm forever grateful for the priceless contribution Jon has made to me, my organization, and the people we coach. Every salesperson in my organization will have to read this book."

**Jeffrey T. Sooey, Founder, Coaches Training Blog community**

"Jon Berghoff has put together a must read for every business owner looking to STEP UP! and take sales to the next level. *Cutting Edge Sales* is the perfect balance of information and inspiration."

**Daniel Grissom, Author of the National Bestselling Book, *STEP UP!***

"Jon knows that your number one skill in business and in life is your ability to sell. We know that the toughest sell of all is selling your own "Little Voice." His information is critical to understanding how to control your income and have the lifestyle you want and deserve."

**— Blair Singer, Bestselling author of *SalesDogs*, *The ABC's of Building a Business Team that Wins* and *Little Voice Mastery***

"AWESOME! I couldn't put it down! So many great, real-world stories, so much first-person insight, so many engaging, non-stop interesting tidbits, I was underlining and highlighting all night. CUTTING EDGE SALES reads like an action suspense novel for anyone hungry for the answers to success in selling. Cut yourself some slack – buy it and read it today!"

**— Bill Guertin, Chief Enthusiasm Officer (CEO) of The 800-Pound Gorilla and Author of *The 800-Pound Gorilla of Sales***

"Cutting Edge Sales is sensational! Brilliant, both in its riveting content and the raw and real world accounts of what it takes to succeed. The wisdom in these pages should be required reading for everyone in sales. And the manner in which the contributors 'stepped up' to make Cutting Edge Sales a charitable project - priceless!"

**— Ben Gay III, THE CLOSERS, www.BFG3.com**

# Table of Contents

# Foreword
# What Do You Want To Be When You Grow Up?

### Jeffrey Gitomer

That's a question that you're asked more than 100 times before you reach your high school graduation. Answers given range anywhere from doctor or lawyer, to teacher or nurse. When you were asked, all kinds of answers were forthcoming - with the exception of one.

No one (including you) ever said, "I want to be a salesman."

But the reality is, within everyone's scholastic career they're asked in one way or another to *go sell something*. Cookies, candy bars, tickets, book covers, wrapping paper - you name it, there's a scout troop or a school fundraiser and stuff to sell.

Most kids just go to their parents and their Aunt Nelly and Uncle John, sell a half-a-dozen items, turn in their money and forget about it until next year's fundraiser.

But some kids, in the spirit of winning, go all out. They don't just sell to their family; they go out in the community, knock on doors, call on merchants and try to win the sales contest.

These contest winners go on to be achievers, not necessarily as salespeople, but with the new found confidence that they got by interacting successfully with people, persuading those people to buy something and ultimately winning the prize.

When you think about it, children learn the art and the science of persuasion and getting their way at a very early age – crying, asking whining, begging, even throwing a tantrum in order to get what they want. You could almost say they are "naturals" at getting their way – primitive, but effective methods. If you have a child you know exactly what I'm talking about.

Young children have a parental closing ratio of somewhere around 100%.

All of this salesmanship and persuasion took place with little or no training - just a natural ability, desire, passion and enthusiasm of a kid on a mission.

I started selling door-to-door when I was seven years old. By the time I went to college, I knew I was going into business for myself, but I had no idea how vital a role salesmanship and selling skills played in becoming a success.

When I was asked to write the foreword for this book, I was eager and elated. Cutco knives and the leadership of the company are dedicated to helping young people gain selling skills and the self-confidence that sales success breeds. Inside are stories of people who cut their teeth (so to speak) in the knife business - selling from kitchen table to kitchen table.

Two of the authors of the book – Jon Berghoff and John Ruhlin – are classic examples of "growing up Cutco." They started at a young age, invested in themselves (bought the starter kit), learned and studied the science of selling through Cutco training, and became so successful, that they have documented their examples and strategies in this book.

Cutco, for those unfamiliar, is a company dedicated to helping young people succeed by teaching them the science of selling, the art of persuasion, the value of a quality product and the pride of personal achievement. And they've done it hundreds of thousands of times.

I met John Ruhlin at a seminar event for a large seed company. John is the founder and CEO of a successful marketing and promotion business that specializes in (what else) Cutco knives. His passion is not only to succeed; it's to influence young people in transition to catch the same fire he caught, the fire to achieve through direct selling.

Jon Berghoff is a rising star in business and life. As a Cutco salesman he broke company records, moved to the health club industry and broke sales records there too – all before the age of 24. Now a successful businessman, ironman marathoner, coach and citizen of humanity, Jon has a passion for helping others, a passion that led him to writing this book.

The other 14 contributing authors are people who HAVE DONE IT. No theory, just the facts from the people who have made the sales, delivered the knives and banked the money. Lots of it.

If you are contemplating selling of any kind – especially direct selling – this is THE book to read, study and implement.

*You will learn:*
- Why direct selling is the best way to start
- Actual strategies and techniques that you can implement immediately.
- The preparation needed for success – today and tomorrow.
- The persistence, persuasion, presentation skills and the process of procuring a purchase order.
- The self-confidence that's bred by making sales.
- The belief system that goes along with a successful sales career
- The pride of accomplishment

Not only is this book a gem, but the authors have decided to give back by donating the profits to charity. They have learned that by giving, they are rewarded far beyond success. They are fulfilled.

I am speaking to you as an author, a trainer and a very successful salesman who learned my most valuable lessons in sales and life while direct selling in high school and college – baby pictures and encyclopedias – in peoples homes – cold and warm calls – acceptance and rejection – highs and lows – making my own income based on my own ability to persuade others.

This book is the gateway to that insight in the 21st century. It's cutting edge and realistic. It's eye-opening information that's on the money – your money.

The only variable is your ability to take advantage of this information and slice your own piece of the American dream. (Make sure you use a Cutco knife when you do.)

Jeffrey Gitomer
Author of *The Sales Bible, The Little Red Book of Selling*
and seven other best selling books.

# Introduction
# The Cutting Edge

Jon Berghoff

On a beautiful summer afternoon, twenty-five years ago, two young men who were friends applied for two different sales positions.

They were very much alike, these two young men. Both had never held a sales position before. Both were ready and willing to work hard. Both were personable. And both were enlivened by ambitious goals for the future.

Recently, these two men had lunch to discuss their now 25 years in sales. They were still very much alike. Both were happily married. Both had two children. Both, it turned out, had gone on to sell various products throughout their careers.

But there was a difference.

One of the men was now a local office manager, performing at a frustrating, mediocre level. The other was a successful entrepreneur, fulfilled by his place in the world and flowing with the abundance to now give back on a grand scale.

## What Made the Difference?

Have you ever been curious about what makes this kind of difference in people's lives?

It isn't necessarily education, background or motivation. It isn't that one person wants success and the other doesn't.

In the case of the two young men, it was something that most people would never guess - the difference was that one of them began their career selling Cutco Cutlery and the other did not. Let me explain.

Since 1949, a growing culture of Cutco Cutlery salespeople has been quietly grooming our nation's youth to be the next generation of CEO's, philanthropists and entrepreneurial success stories.

Cutco Cutlery has been attracting the attention of universities, text books and is an example of an exceptional training ground for sales professionals, business owners and entrepreneurs.

## Why This Book?

For the first time in manuscript form, I've gathered together 14 former and current Cutco Cutlery sales professionals – with over $300 million combined in Cutco Cutlery sales – to collaborate and share their best insights and ideas. If you are a sales professional, business owner or entrepreneur, the wisdom between your hands is bound to inspire you.

As you will soon read, many of the authors left Cutco to make incredible contributions to our world - some through successful businesses, some through philanthropic efforts and some through different forms of charity and public service.

I hand-selected each contributing author and organized the process of putting this book together, from concept to completion. Each author, through their involvement in this book, acknowledges that selling Cutco was instrumental, if not the number one factor, in their future endeavors and successes.

It should be noted that Cutco Cutlery has no affiliation, influence or involvement in the development of this manuscript. Each of the contributing authors independently chose to deliver the best insights and ideas they could, to motivate, instruct and inspire the current and future generations of sales professionals, business owners and entrepreneurs.

## A Unique Philanthropic Twist

This project was inspired largely by a private meeting between myself and Dr. Ivan Misner, founder of BNI, the world's largest referral organization. Dr. Misner founded BNI on the philosophy that when you show up with the intention of giving, you ultimately walk away having gained. The BNI motto is literally "Givers Gain®."

Following this meeting, I sat in the hotel lobby and thought to myself, how could I create a book project that would not only give back through the powerful lessons that were taught, but also allow the book the ability to give back to charitable causes around the world. I decided that while reaching out to the potential authors for this book, I would ask if they would be willing to donate some portion of their share of the royalties to a charity of their choice.

I'm proud, grateful and moved to share with you what happened. Each contributing author of this book, unanimously, and without knowing what the other authors would agree to, offered to give 100% of their share of royalties, to a charity or cause of their choosing. Each of these authors made it possible for this book to become, in and of itself, a philanthropic project. You will find the charities they are supporting listed in the back of the book.

I'm not sure if anything more needs to be said about the people in this book, who they are, and what they represent. Nevertheless, here is what you can expect from *Cutting Edge Sales*.

- **Dan Casetta**, who was also my first manager with Cutco and a long-time mentor, passes along wisdom that has recently sparked a business partner of mine to call Dan a "Modern Day Dale Carnegie". You will find in his chapter some of the most powerful, precise and practical advice on influencing others. You will instantly see why his office is the most prolific in Cutco sales history.

- **Carl Drew** shares, for the first time in writing, an account of his adventure climbing K2, considered one of the most dangerous mountains in the world. Carl masterfully connects lessons learned in sales with the application of these lessons in his story. This chapter is guaranteed to leave you riveted.

- With over $200 million in career sales and 6 of 7 consecutive regional championships, **Brad Britton** was a history-maker and world-shaker in the Cutco world. I personally learned from Brad while he was with Cutco, and his chapter reminds me of why he was, and always will be, a great contributor on this planet. Brad's chapter will inspire you to look inwards. His ability to deliver profound ideas with simplicity is truly enlightening.

- What would it take to go from no one to number one? **John Ruhlin** did it by cracking the code to relationship-building on the highest levels. What will shock you is how easy it is to implement the same ideas that made John the number one all time sales rep for Cutco.

- Very few people have dedicated their lives to a cause the way **Jon Vroman** has dedicated himself to growing and learning. When looking at all the ways Jon changes lives, they stem from his passion to grow and build relationships, which he talks about in his chapter. What is magical about Jon's chapter is his ability to give tangible, easy to implement and instant, yet profound, life-changing ideas.

- There are few skills more helpful than being able to listen to your intuition and using what you hear to attract the results you want. This is especially true of sales people and business owners who often work independently. **Fi Mazanke** has not only taught these skills as a successful leadership coach, but she writes about them from a place of personal experience in her chapter. She will inspire you to ask for and get exactly what you want out of life.

- Do passion and entrepreneurship go together? **Ranjeet Pawar** thinks so and when you see how successful his passion has made him as an entrepreneur, you will want to learn his ways. His chapter will drive you to see and create your life as an artistic masterpiece, to be the best and to reach beyond what you thought was possible.

- Many have wondered what the correlation is between selling and leading. **Jerry Liu** tackles the connection between the two and does so with an unforgettable metaphor that will captivate your attention. The clarity and focus in this chapter makes it no secret why Jerry was a national champion manager for Cutco.

- Goal setting is a topic commonly taught. Learning about goal setting from somebody who has the profound experience of conducting over 13,000 personal training sessions is not as common. **John Edwin** shares his stories and lessons learned from his successful personal training business. His track record alone makes him the expert on this topic.

- I regularly argue that selling is always happening. **Paulette Tucciarone** confirms this in her awe-inspiring accounts of transferring her objection-handling skills to the do or die – literally – in the arena of being a doctor. Paulette also shares a one of a kind perspective on emotional intelligence that will leave you thinking.

- If you were required to pack your bags tonight and move your business to a brand new territory tomorrow, reading **John Israel's** chapter might be the single best action to start up and succeed in business. John presents lessons on starting and building relationships the right way. You will be swimming in referrals when you apply John's advice.

- Our time is worth money and there is no better person to talk about the relationship between the two than **Adam Stock,** financial planner. Adam's chapter is an engaging, detailed look into the often miscalculated task of delegating. The clarity you receive on what, why and when you should delegate will liberate your business.

- What if your customers and clients sold themselves on your behalf? Value what **Jason Scheckner** shares about consultative selling and this just might happen. The strategies and tips that Jason reveals are precisely what have consistently made him a national sales champion in multiple industries.

- Coming from a top producer who simultaneously doubled his annual sales report, wrote a bestselling book and successfully launched a new career all in the same year, **Hal Elrod's** chapter is full of powerful strategies to transform your business. In addition to laying out an easy to follow step-by-step plan for getting to the next level, Hal also shares unique insights into how to leverage the power of accountability.

## Now, What Should You Do?

As you read through this book, you will find that the main points from each chapter are compiled as Summary Points. Take the lessons to heart, put the summary points to the test and challenge yourself to get to another level. You will also find a Bonus Gift in the back of the book to further your learning, development and success as a sales professional. We hope you enjoy.

Go now to www.cuttingedgesalesbook.com/bonusgifts to claim your FREE Bonus Gifts.

I sincerely hope you enjoy the wisdom between these pages.

Kind Regards,

*Jon Berghoff*

Jon Berghoff's interactive trainings have reached over 75,000 students live and over 300 business owners across more than 50 professions, through over 3,500 private coaching calls. Prior to becoming a trainer, coach and consultant, Jon was the youngest and fastest ever inducted into the Cutco Hall of Fame, breaking 17 weekly, monthly and annual records along the way. Jon went on to parallel his success managing sales in the health club and wellness industry, building a championship sales organization from scratch. Jon met the love of his life, his wife Mara, while volunteering for the Front Row Foundation, and he regularly competes as an amateur endurance athlete, running 100 mile ultra marathons to raise money for the Front Row Foundation. Visit Jon at www.geconnection.com.

# Influence
# From The Inside Out

## Jon Berghoff

## Making History

Wow! A historical election, a once in a millennium economic crisis, housing busts, the energy crisis. Pick your passion, pick your poison; history is being made at every turn, right now. War, going green, Brittany Spears, I-Phones, you name it; we can say with certainty that this period of time will be referred to as a turning point for humanity.

Your reason for opening this book may not have been to make history, but at a time when so many others are finding comfort in standing on the sidelines, placing blame, making excuses, and sharing in the fear inflated rhetoric of today's business economy, I find it even more worthy of a reminder to stand out. Not only does the world need and want business leaders, but the rewards for doing so will rise, while so many others act in fear, during turbulent times.

Here are some of the most important questions to ask yourself right now:

- How are you making your own history right now?

- Are you creating your own defining moments every single day?

- What are you doing that will make this time in your life worth telling your grandchildren about one day?

- How are you rising above mediocrity, the masses and fear-based thinking to create your own rhythm of success?

I want to acknowledge you for picking up this book, because whether intentional or not, the purchase of this book will change history for those whom its royalties are supporting through charitable causes. I honor you for your personal journey, and look forward to learning from you one day soon. From one salesperson, business owner and entrepreneur to another, I sincerely hope the content of this book will provide you with the tools, ideas and inspiration to help you shape your own personal and/or professional history.

## Every Master Was Once…

A disaster.

That's what I was. At the age of 17, I was on the verge of getting "permanently uninvited" or as most people know it, expelled from my high school. I allegedly didn't learn the way my teachers taught. I simply didn't value my education at the level I should have.

The story I learned to tell myself was that I couldn't focus, wasn't a good learner and couldn't fit in. Doctors told me it was okay to believe that I had a problem focusing. I was rejected from every university I applied to. It only made sense to keep believing my story. I wasn't destined for anything great.

The true turning point and defining moment came when a friend of mine introduced me to an opportunity selling Cutco kitchen knives. I had never sold anything and knew nothing about kitchen products.

I had no reason to be selling knives. So, of course, I quit my job at the local golf course, and signed up to sell Cutco knives.

During the interview, they presented the pay structure. I would get paid, not based on what I wanted or somebody else's perception of my value, but strictly on what I deserved, or the results I showed.

"This is how life works," I thought to myself.

Life responds to deserve, not want or need. I tuned in.

My first manager and mentor, Dan Casetta (also a contributor to this book), taught me a valuable lesson that tapped into a seed that my parents had been planting for many years.

"Your income will seldom exceed your level of personal development," Dan said to me, one week into the job.

My father always taught me to learn something from everything, and now, I was finally seeing the connection between knowledge and wealth - the connection between learning today and earning tomorrow.

## Looking Back

A decade later, I look back at what Dan's wisdom, combined with my Cutco experience, has brought me.

With Cutco, I became the national sales champion my first full year in the business and went on to be the youngest and fastest person to be inducted into the company Hall of Fame. After leaving Cutco, I paralleled my success in two more, completely unrelated industries, and have now taught my life and business lessons to tens of thousands of small business owners and sales professionals across the globe.

As previously mentioned, I've also been told I was an idiot, unable to learn – let alone teach – and not a good learner. Just reminding you that where you have been, where you are, and what others say about you, need not reflect where you are going.

I've had over 5,500 customers, clients and prospects say "yes" after being asked to buy something that I or one of my teams was selling. Every lesson I've learned - whether I was selling kitchen knives, corporate health club memberships, high end furniture, websites, software, real estate or my own coaching and training services - falls under one very important category: Influence.

## Influence Is an "Inside-Out" Job

Beyond my own successes and failures, through the careful observation of the most successful sales professionals in the world, I've noticed a commonality in perspective on influence. Great influencers - whether they be the salesperson, manager, leader, entrepreneur, parent, coach, trainer or speaker – place an equal importance on their ability to not only influence others, but also to influence themselves.

In my seminars, I often remind my students that influence – in selling, managing, teaching, leading, attracting customers - is an energy sport. The person with the most powerful energy - certainty, conviction, passion, enthusiasm – usually walks away with the sale. The energy of influence starts from within. Remember, we can't give what we don't have.

As great influencers put importance on both the self and others, when they approach influence, neither is more or less important. They both play a role in every success and failure that we create. They both deserve equal attention in our quest to improve as sales professionals, business owners, teachers, trainers, coaches, managers, and leaders - as influencers.

## Influencing the Self:
## Rights, Responsibilities, Realities

## Success Is Your Birthright – With a Catch

Life operates in seasons. As people, in our businesses, in the economy, in relationships, in nature, seasons are continually changing. We move from spring through the summer into autumn and winter. When in the winter of life, sometimes we need critical reminders that allow us to influence the self to take action.

Whether you are currently harvesting great success, or working through a personal or professional winter, you might enjoy the following reminder. It has motivated me many times.

In 1910, Wallace Wattles reminded us in "The Science of Getting Rich" that we not only have the right to be successful, but that the world wants us to be successful. How do we know this?

It's simple.

If you were to envision yourself successful, prosperous and wealthy beyond your wildest imagination as a result of running a successful business, think about how you got there. To be really successful, what would you have done along the way? Do you see it yet? Do you see why the world wants you to be wealthy?

If you were to walk backwards from your future vision of wild success, notice that in order to get there, you had to have helped many others along the way, by creating immense value, whether it be through your product, ideas, leadership, teachings or services.

As Zig Ziglar taught long ago, "If you help enough people get what they want, you'll have whatever you want." Success – wealth, riches, prosperity – is not only your birthright, but the world wants it for you.

This is why it's simple - your personal success will always be in proportion to the value that you provide to the world, and that's the catch. You have the right to be successful, if you give something in return.

## The Responsibility Choice:
## None, Some or Total Ownership

The fact that you are reading this book says that you, an influencer – salesperson, business owner, entrepreneur, coach or leader - are likely NOT in the category of 'no ownership,' meaning you take no responsibility for your results. That leaves two choices: 'Some ownership' or 'total ownership.'

Most of us have been conditioned to only take "some ownership" over our results. You may notice that whenever a controversial political, economic or social issue crops up, people are quick to place blame. But remember, fault is a low intelligence concept.

Earl Nightingale said in the 1950s, "To be successful, we must look at what everybody else is doing and consider doing the opposite." Look at those who blame others. Look at those who blame the economy. Look at those who blame their product, their circumstances, their family, their background, their shortcomings, the weather, Paris Hilton and everything else they can think up, for poor results.

Consider doing the opposite. Consider joining the few who really do choose to take total ownership over their results. You will be given the riches that the many who only take "some ownership" will never find.

Be willing to own ALL your results, good and bad. Great presenters succeed by intentionally crafting their messages and when they fail, they convert objection and rejection into the perfect opportunity to redraft their message. They own the result.

Be willing to own ALL the results of your team, as a leader, good and bad. Great leaders look across the hall when things go well and say "you did it" and look inside when things don't go well and say "I did it." They own the result, especially when things don't go well.

Bottom line, as my good friend Hal Elrod (also a contributor to this book) taught me, to the degree that you take responsibility for everything in your life, you will be able to change anything in your life.

Great influencers settle for nothing but total responsibility.

## Lessons about Reality:
## Learned At Extreme Angles

I'm a fanatical motorcyclist, so much so that I've hired, on more than one occasion, the best advanced riding instructor my money could find: Jim Ford, the Zen Motorcycle Man.

Why does this matter to you?

I've found, with great appreciation, that many of the lessons Jim teaches me about high performance motorcycling, while we wind through the beautiful, yet technical twists and curves of our classroom – the roads of the Appalachian mountains – seem to remind me of the lessons that I've found critical to selling and business success.

At high speeds and tight lean angles, trying to fly a 500-plus pound machine along the perfect line of a twisty curve, at precisely the right RPM, while also being fully present to the conditions, risks and dangers of the environment, can be stimulating beyond what words can describe. The need for constant mental focus combined with the battle between the little voices in my head when things get challenging, bring me back to the lessons I learned selling.

One of the most profound, yet simple lessons, is the following idea: we go where we look.

When Jim reminds me through our in-helmet, wireless communication system, that I simply need to look where I want to go, I know that this simple advice has saved my butt from allowing fear – False Expectation Appearing Real – to overcome my ability to stay focused and not bail out of a tight turn.

It is true in motorcycling, as it is in sales and in business, that we run the risk of getting tense, losing focus and imagining what we don't want, whenever we sense we are heading into danger.

You've probably heard the idea that what we focus on expands. What we appreciate will appreciate. It's all the same lesson.

Here is the bottom line: In sales and in business – and motorcycling - there are challenges. They are inevitable. If you are on a path with no challenges, the rewards probably won't be very exciting either. The greatest distinction between those who grow from the challenges and those who shrink – or those who crash vs. those who glide through them- is where they are looking while they are in the middle of it all. This is influencing the Self at its greatest.

Where do you look? Do you look at the opportunity or the challenge? Do you see how you can grow, learn, and expand from each set back? Challenges never leave us in the same place. We either move forward or backward – but never stay the same. The difference between which direction you go… is where you look.

## Another Application of Jim's Lesson

I would go out on a limb and say that Jim's teaching – you go where you look – could even be used to predict your likelihood of succeeding in the "new economy" in less than two minutes. This is a great self-study in how you regularly influence yourself. All you have to do is pay attention to how you feel when I make the following statement: "In this book you will be given one idea that will absolutely change your life or your business forever."

How did you respond to this statement? Did you "move away from it" with doubt, hesitation, skepticism or pessimism? Or…

Did you "move towards it" with proactive anticipation, energy to take action, anticipation and enthusiasm? (I'm hoping this is the more likely option.)

The reason I ask is because of one simple Life Principle: How you do one thing is often how you do everything. How does this apply to the above statement that I made?

The above statement is a reflection of how you approach potential opportunities. I said that you will be given one idea in this book that will change your life, which was nothing more than an example of a potential opportunity. Regardless of what is in this book, your conditioned response to the statement (moving towards or away from), is generally reflective of how you approach any and every new opportunity.

Why does all this matter? In the "new economy" (down economy, recession, depression… whatever you want to call it), only those who seek – move towards, embrace and get excited about- the opportunities within the challenges, will actually thrive, let alone survive.

As I shared with a client recently, if people are jumping out of the window because the economy is freaking them out, I simply need to influence myself to focus on being the guy who sells the mattresses that they land on. Get it yet?

Remember, where you look, you will go.

## Influencing Others:
## Lessons from Fiji Water, Late Night Television, My Wife

### Every Book is Judged By its Cover

If I took a bottle of Fiji water and I asked you how much somebody would pay for the water, you would have to answer somewhere between $2 and $3. If I took the same water, poured it into a generic, Styrofoam cup and asked you, "How much would somebody pay for this water?", the answer now shifts, likely to free.

Here is the critical question: What determines the value? Is it the content or the packaging of the content - the context - that determines the "perceived value" of the water? This is a big picture lesson on influence that I apply to every type of communication.

As a leader or manager, for example, the end value of every important conversation you want to have will be determined not only by the content of the conversation, but by the context that you set, as you bring somebody into the conversation.

Do you prepare ahead of time? Are you sending out an agenda before the meeting? Do you have your critical points in writing to hand out during the meeting? Do you take interruptions during the meeting? Do you acknowledge the thoughts, feelings, experiences of your audience before you start the meeting?

Your answers to these questions are all about the kind of context you set. Everything you do and/or communicate before and at the beginning of every conversation sets up the context for the rest of the conversation. Being prepared, not allowing interruptions, looking somebody in the eyes, creating ways for ideas to be documented and tracked, are all examples of strengthening the value of your conversations.

You sell an expensive, high dollar service or product. Are you waiting until your prospect objects or are you conscientiously building into your conversation – at the very beginning – why your price is actually appreciated by your current customers? Are you allowing your prospect to mention your competitors, or do you intentionally bring up your competitors – before the prospect – and talk about why they are great, and also why your customers appreciate you above your competitors. Do you see the difference when you set the right context? This is influence in action.

In a selling situation, look at every objection as a learning experience. A consistent objection is a symptom of a presentation that should be adjusted. View the adjustment as a way of setting the context, through which your customer will see the content – your product – a little differently. Dan Casetta does a fantastic job in his chapter of talking about "framing," which is an example of setting the context.

How you bring somebody into a conversation – regardless of setting - determines the value of and perception of the rest of the conversation. Think carefully about the way you package your every communication. People do judge books by their covers.


## Why People Buy

Turn on the television late at night; what do you see?

That's right, you'll see infomercials. Often these infomercials fall into one of two categories: health products or money-making schemes. You know the ones I'm talking about.

Let's talk about the money-making schemes.

You've seen them. Bob the plumber comes on to give a testimonial about how he went from rags to riches. Photos of fancy cars, swimming pools and people with great tans rotate in the background. This is a billion dollar industry. But what is the industry?

When you look at the money-making schemes, do you actually know what it is that they are selling? No, you don't. They rarely, if ever, actually reveal what it is that they are selling. So what is the lesson here?

People don't buy because they understand what the infomercials are selling. They buy because they feel understood.

Think about it. Whether you are selling insurance, cleaning products, homes, technology, ideas, an opportunity, lemonade or companies - people and businesses are the same. They want to be understood. Some questions to consider:

1.  Do you understand your prospects? What do they really want? Do they want your product or do they want all the benefits that come with your product? Do they want the features of your product or the emotional benefits? Do you really know your prospects, your target market, inside and out?

    This is a critical lesson in influence. Know more about your prospects than anybody else. Read what they read, eat what they eat, talk the way they talk, hang out where they hang out. Enter their world, both mentally, and physically, and you're ability to sell will skyrocket.

2.  Are you proving to your prospects that you know what it is like to be them? Just knowing them is only half the battle. Now you must prove that you know them. It is okay if you can articulate, even better than your prospect, what it is like to be them. They will appreciate it.

Bottom line: Begin every conversation, relationship, presentation by making sure those in front of you feel understood. Acknowledge what they are thinking, how they feel, what they fear, believe, get frustrated by and what they deeply want.

I have studied the highest paid public speakers and trainers in the world. Their ability to acknowledge their audience, align with them, and show they understand them is always their first priority.

Back when President Obama was in a heated race with Hillary Clinton for the Democratic nomination, I was standing in line at a local pizza place, watching the television screen during the opening of one of their debates. At the time, they were practically neck and neck and John Edwards had just bowed out of the race.

Obama made a single comment and I immediately sent an email to my buddy Hal and my wife Mara, reading, "Barack is our next president."

I saw him implementing, with perfection, the topic we just talked about. Here is what happened:

Obama opened his comments by first acknowledging the supporters of John Edwards. This was brilliant because Obama knew that with Edwards out of the race, many of his supporters would now be up for grabs. It was his very first public comment since Edwards ducked out and it was aimed directly at those supporters.

They were acknowledged. They were understood. They were respected. Barack knew Edward's supporters wanted to be understood before they needed to understand him. He won the nomination, and ultimately a historic bid for presidency.

## Influence Lessons from My Wife

My wife Mara, who also worked for Cutco, is one of the greatest developers of people I have ever met. She is a great leader, and an incredible person of influence.

Mara was known in the company for her magical ability to lead, inspire and attract great people and it is no surprise she is a member of the Cutco Hall of Fame as a manager. The value in what Mara knows about influence transcends sales management and applies to any and every area of influence.

So, what is Mara's secret?

When I ask Mara why was she able to attract, retain and develop leaders at the highest levels of performance, she always replies with one simple answer, "People want to feel good."

Do people feel good around you? Do you make others smile? Do others want to be around you? This might sound like a step backward from "high level" sales training, but at the very core, this is as important as it gets.

At the end of the day, people don't buy products, they buy people. They buy you. They buy how they feel around you

People are starving for recognition, a compliment, a laugh or somebody who can sincerely make them feel good. Don't overlook the power of this. I would go as far as saying that whether you sell a product, service, idea or opportunity, your mission should revolve around making others feel good. Thank people in as many ways as possible. Do it verbally, in writing, in private and in public. My good friend Jon Vroman (also a contributor to this book) is a master at thanking others, and talks about it in his chapter.

It sounds simple, but it isn't always easy.

What is the secret? It starts with making sure that you feel good yourself.

Remember, influence is the process of transformation. You can only transform others to the degree that you can transform yourself. You can't give what you don't have. They will only feel good about you, what you are selling or just life, to the degree they see you feel good about yourself, your product or even life in general.

If you find yourself in a winter of life, ask what you can be grateful for. What you appreciate appreciates. As you focus on what you do have, instead of what you don't have, you will find a joy that will end up reflecting in those around you.


## Putting It Together:
## Balance Isn't the Answer

As a coach, teacher, trainer, speaker, salesperson, manager, business owner, I wear many hats of influence. I know what it's like to win, and I know what it's like to struggle. I've been the person at the top, and

I've been the person with a total lack of confidence in what I was doing. Would it surprise you if I told you that I was both of those people at the same time?

The big problem isn't learning how to influence ourselves to be more successful, or discovering the newest ways to influence our team, our customers, or the people around us. The greatest challenge we all face is in succeeding without sacrificing other areas of our lives - succeeding without giving up being fulfilled.

Have you ever had this happen? You are working, but thinking about playing? Then you are playing, but thinking about working? That's the worst feeling in the world. Regardless of success, that's not fulfillment.

The problem isn't in finding balance in our lives. I'm a big believer that if you pay attention to great achievers, they often have *intentional imbalance.* Even those who are fulfilled experience this. They spend completely disproportionate periods of time to build a business, follow a passion, or learn their craft. So if balance isn't the answer, than what is?

Being present. If you want to get more out of each experience, deepen your relationships, multiply your effectiveness, increase your ability to influence others, and find more joy in each moment, then be there. Turn off the phones, shut the door, quiet the noise. Look at whatever is in front of you – the person, the meeting, the speech, the phone call, the task at hand – and be one hundred percent present.

This is the ultimate tool of influence, the secret to understanding what each moment calls for, the pathway to really listening, deeply, to the problems, needs, and desires of your customers, your team, your family, and yourself. Be here, right now. Influence happens by understanding what you can give, by owning your results, by looking where you want to go, by setting the context, through understanding whoever is in front of you, and feeling what those around you feel. And all of this happens, in the present moment.

**Summary Points**

- Make history by rising above mediocrity.

- Being a person of influence requires focus on influencing both the Self and Others.

- Claim your birthright to success by providing value to the world.

- Take ownership over everything around you, without exception.

- You go in the direction where you look.

- Set the context to control the value of the content of your conversations.

- People don't buy because they understand what you are selling, but because they feel understood.

- People want to buy from and be around people who make them feel good.

- Rather than trying to be perfectly balanced, focus on being present, to get the most out of every moment.

Dan Casetta has been one of the most successful members of the Cutco/Vector organization for the past 20 years. He has won five Silver Cups for being the #1 manager in the company for the year. His San Jose sales office is the most prolific sales team in the history of the company and Dan has become one of the most sought-after speakers at company events across the nation. He has produced more than $63 million of sales for the company and is a member of the Cutco/Vector Hall of Fame. Dan is a huge sports fan, loves to travel and also enjoys playing poker.

# Precision Language
# Great Influencers Know What to Say

### Dan Casetta

Have you ever been around someone who always seemed like they knew what to say?

Some people just seem to have an innate ability to think on their feet and come up with the right words at the right time. This is more a function of understanding human psychology and being quick-witted than anything I can teach in a brief chapter on verbal skills.

However, there are some basic verbal skills that help make more of a connection with others, and open up their ears so that we can have more influence. In the pages that follow, I will share some of the most important verbal skills I have ever learned. Some of these are basic. Others will be more advanced. But ALL of these are truly valuable skills that can help you have a powerful influence on the people in your circle of friends and associates.

## Why You Should Pay Attention to This Stuff

During my career as a sales manager with the Cutco organization, I had a 10-year stretch in which my sales team broke over 100 company records. At one point, we held the national records for one week, one month, one campaign (4 months), and one year in team sales. I became the highest-producing Division Manager in the history of the company in terms of total sales from a single division.

In addition, I developed a number of other people who achieved national champion status in the company, including one young man who, at 18-years old, set national records for one week, one month, one campaign, and one year in sales for an individual. That young man is Jon Berghoff, co-author and mastermind behind this project.

I know how to sell. I know how to influence people. And I have developed these skills in a wide range of other people over the years. Those who have a profound ability to move the world around them all display certain characteristics.

I call these characteristics the Skills of Influence. I have identified five key factors that contribute to one's ability to influence. In my upcoming book entitled, *5 Critical Skills of Influence*, I will share these five factors and go into detail on the development and use of each of the skills.

In this chapter, I will discuss the most obvious and prevalent skill of the master influencer, that being precision language.

## Something You Know But Don't Do

The first verbal skill of great influencers is the use of people's names. Dale Carnegie wrote "The sweetest sound in any language is the sound of one's own name."

When a leader in your life knows and uses your name, you immediately feel better around them. This feeling opens your mind and your ears to what they have to say. So, it's important for all of us to learn to use the names of the people with whom we are surrounded on a daily basis. This requires that we become sincerely interested in people.

If you are sincerely interested in someone, then you WANT to know their name. You pay attention when they offer it, fully intending to remember them so that you can use their name later in the conversation, when parting ways or at a future meeting.

> *When a leader in your life knows and uses your name, you immediately feel better around them. This feeling opens your mind and your ears to what they have to say.*

Applications of this concept:

### 1. Salespeople dealing with a customer

While dealing with a potential customer, a salesperson should develop the habit of frequently dropping the prospect's name into the conversation. Using their name personalizes your presentation and also grabs and/or holds attention. The customer might be drifting off thinking of their next objection or something completely un-related to what you are discussing. When you drop their name into the conversation, it immediately grabs them.

### 2. Managers working with subordinates

If you are a manager of any sort, knowing the names of everyone under your guidance is critical to your relationship-building. Any time you greet someone by name, it deepens your connection and immediately grabs them. Some people will feel good, just because you know their name. People who feel good about themselves (as we will discuss later) perform better in your organization.

### 3. Teachers or coaches

We've all had teachers who just pointed at someone and others who took great pains to learn everyone's name as quickly as possible. Which did you like better and respect more? Learning the names of as many pupils as possible garners immediate respect and attention and recognizing them by name for excellent participation increases rapport and makes the pupils more open to the leader's influence.

Sometimes, I'll run training classes with 50 or more people. During introductions, I'll make a seating chart to help me learn names. By the end of one day, I'll usually have them all down. Believe me, it matters.

## 4. Day to day dealings with people

Everywhere I go, I make an effort to learn the names of the people I deal with. Whether it be a customer service representative on the phone who offers their name in opening the conversation, a sales clerk in a store wearing (or not wearing) a name tag or the waiter or waitress serving me in a restaurant, I pay attention and remember their name. So few of the people they deal with use their name in conversation that doing so sets you apart from the crowd. Rapport is deepened and your influence is increased.

This added level of influence can often be to your benefit and at least makes for a more satisfying interaction for you and the people around you. When it's appropriate (and it almost always is) ask to know the name of the people you deal with and call them by name during your interaction.

## Dale Carnegie Didn't Mention This

Another tool of language we can utilize to more powerfully affect others is a compliment. Everyone likes to receive a compliment, whether it be for a job well done, a nice car, a new haircut, a sharp outfit or anything you see that you like about them.

Several things are important about giving compliments.

First, a compliment must be sincere. Don't try offering up compliments that you don't feel are sincere. People will see through that and then wonder what else you will lie about. Thus, your influence would be compromised severely.

But if you do recognize something you like about someone, tell them. Learn to offer compliments in a manner that conveys sincerity and interest. After stating a compliment, it's always a good idea to offer up a reason supporting the compliment and then ask a relevant question that gets the other person talking.

For example, the following:

- That's a really nice car. I really love the way the interior looks. What made you decide to get this model?

- You always wear such nice outfits for these events. Your sport coat and slacks are very professional; yet they show off your personality better than a plain suit. I've never seen you in this coat; is it new?

- You did a great job last week. I really admire your consistency. It's great to have someone on the team that I know I can always count on. What's something you have been doing each week that has helped you succeed at such a high level recently?

Practice this method whenever you offer up a compliment to someone.

## You'll Thank Me For This Tip

Another verbal tool we can use to enhance our influence is the tool of appreciation. Merely saying thank you for all the little things people do around us, makes others feel good about us. And the better they feel about us, the more they like us, the greater our connection with them. This makes the things we say and do have more power in their eyes.

William James once wrote, "The deepest principle in human nature is the craving to be appreciated." Note that he used the word "craving." Humans have a deep desire to feel appreciated. When you meet this need in another person, you are strengthening your connection with them.

Any time I have any transaction with another person, I take a moment to smile and sincerely thank them for their efforts. Again, this is something that so few people are used to that it really sets you apart from the crowd. Anything that makes your interaction with others more memorable will certainly serve to benefit you in the future.

But even without any sort of self-serving thoughts of the future, making people feel good about meeting you and dealing with you is just a better way to live! Smile and thank the grocery store clerk, the bank teller, the flight attendants as you step off the plane and anyone else who serves you, even for a moment.

You'll make them feel better and you'll feel better about yourself. Anything we do to build up others ends up building us as well.

> *The deepest principle in human nature*
> *is the craving to be appreciated.*
> *-- William James*

Teach this philosophy to all employees and you can build a better business. I am often amazed how few people actually take the time to express a sincere thank you to someone patronizing their place of business. Naturally, most employees are just there for their hourly paycheck and don't care that much about the long-term success of the enterprise. But if their employer knew their name and connected with them better, they might care more about the enterprise. (Creating that feeling in your organization is another whole book I could write).

The more you set an example and personally express your gratitude, the more the people around you will do the same.

I often play poker, a great game of skill, and every 60-90 seconds, I get a chance to see this dynamic at work. After most hands, the winning player provides the dealer with a tip, often just $1, sometimes more. Some dealers, recognizing that this is truly an optional gratuity, show appreciation EVERY TIME. I believe their expressions of gratitude (rather than a conveyance of entitlement) create a better feeling with the players in the game, which results in more tips.

I know they don't do it because they want more tips; they do it because they are sincerely grateful. And that's the whole point: expressing your gratitude frequently and sincerely creates a better feeling all around you and subtly increases your influence with others.

On a related note, written thank you notes are one of the single most powerful ways to establish a connection with the people you deal with in your business and personal life. Think about the last time you received a personal thank you note from someone. You may have to think back really far just to remember.

A personal, thank you note is such a powerful way to connect with a customer and set you apart from the other people they deal with. Naturally, a handwritten note is most effective here. However, if you feel you don't want to make the time for this, there are several services you can employ which help expedite the process of sending thank you like www.thankyoucardmagic.com. Check it out, then learn to set your business apart by showing appreciation in your own unique way.

One sales manager in my organization has been teaching others his concept of "appreciation calls." Once a week, he makes a personal phone call to each person on his staff (30+ people) and thanks them for their role on the team in the past week. His people look forward to these calls and often tell him how much MORE he can expect from them in the coming week or as they continue to progress in the organization. What a great way to connect with your team and increase your influence with them!

Remember: "The deepest principle in human nature is the **craving** to be appreciated." Fill that craving by learning to show your appreciation frequently and sincerely.

## The Most Important Thing
## I've Learned About Developing People

Another related language skill that can increase our influence centers around our ability to make people feel important and say things that build the self-image of the people around us.

In my management experience, I've learned that people have a strong tendency to perform according to the image they hold of themselves. I have seen this in sales, in sports, even in relationships.

Watch a person who considers himself to be a terrible golfer. If he goes out and shoots well for 3 or 4 holes, he could be on his way to the best round of his life. But then self-image takes over and brings him back into his own comfortable reality. The end result is usually about what he normally shoots.

A bad bowler who starts with two strikes seldom parlays that start into a solid game. Instead, she merely considers herself to have been "lucky" and that luck runs out in the remaining frames. It's the same way with the people we are leading and developing in our businesses or in our lives. High performance does not build high self-image nearly as much as high self-image builds high performance.

## Which Is True?

> *High performance --> High self-image or*
> *High self-image --> High performance*

How can we use this principle to help us in influencing the people around us?

Well, first, we must recognize that sometimes, initial success comes by accident. Don't assume that just because a new sales rep succeeds right out of the gate that they feel immediate self-confidence and greater motivation. Instead, focus on reinforcing the actions they have taken to experience that early success and the personal characteristics you observe in them that you like.

For example, if you notice that they seem to be a "good student" of your business, taking notes and asking all the right questions, compliment their efforts in that way.

What you recognize gets repeated.

The more they duplicate those same efforts and actions, the more likely they are to continue to sustain success. More importantly, your recognition of them makes them feel good about themselves and builds their confidence and self-image.

If you see someone succeeding early on in a sales setting and you can identify a personal characteristic that you view as one of their strengths, point it out. Anytime I have had a sales rep who seemed to have an immediate ability to connect with people and was seemingly well-liked by everyone, I would tell them that the greatest key to success in sales is likeability, and that with their personality, they were sure to be headed for success.

Again, this type of compliment truly builds a person's self-image and gets them to attribute solid early results to themselves rather than any outside influence or circumstance. It's a way of building someone into a more confident person who expects to succeed.

Confident people who expect to succeed tend to do well at everything they focus on. If you can take someone with some decent initial results, build their confidence and expectations and get them to repeat the actions that have gotten them that initial success, you can turn a solid performer into a superstar. The process of continuing to build their image never stops.

Over my years developing a sales organization, I have learned that it's more important to get people to really believe in themselves than it is to teach them specific sales techniques. Of course, both things are important but, well-trained sales reps who don't feel confident in themselves rarely succeed in the long run, while confident people with a high self-image usually succeed at anything they do. Because they *expect* to succeed, they naturally tend to find the answers to the challenges they encounter.

The process of becoming good at sales (or whatever they are doing) is natural for them. Knowing this, I have always tended to focus my training towards personal development skills and ideas which help build self-image, while also providing a solid foundation of basic sales skills or letting others in my organization provide the sales training while I provide the "life training."

> *Confident people who expect to succeed tend to do well at everything they focus on.*

Building self-image and making people feel important can also be accomplished by involving them in certain key decisions that can affect the group or organization. You are showing that you value them when you get their input. None of us enjoys working with a boss who unilaterally exerts his or her will in every situation. While there is a time to do that, those occasions are few and far between unless you are on a battlefield. You can develop a greater synergy by involving key people in many decisions.

In the long run, this synergy will profoundly increase your influence on them so that when the time comes for you to persuade them to a certain way of thinking, you will more effectively be able to do so.

I have one key person in my organization who has clearly distinguished himself from the rest of my team. He is truly one of the rising stars in our whole company. I like to involve him in the process by asking for his input whenever I have a key decision that will affect our whole division.

I know that as he goes, so goes the rest of my organization. His support is critical. Of course, we usually agree on things, but not always. By getting his input, I am able to make better decisions regarding the direction of our team and I gain his full support (even when we occasionally disagree) and even more importantly, his trust and the trust of my whole team.

My influence with this key person and my whole organization is powerful because I am willing to involve people in key decisions and I make efforts to make them feel important.

Now, on from the "good stuff" to the "really good stuff"...

## Don't Even Question This

One of my favorite language skills is to teach people the use of what I call "quality questions." Quality questions are questions which serve to lead your conversation in a direction toward your ultimate objective: a sale, a commitment to a goal or agreement on any matter.

There are generally two types of questions I teach people to use frequently: "Positive Response Questions" and "Controlled Questions." A Positive Response Question gives the listener a chance to say "yes," to agree or to express interest in what the speaker is offering.

Examples of Positive Response Questions from selling Cutco Cutlery:

- "Can you see how you would use this knife?"

- "Do you understand what that one is for?"

- "Can you see why it's important to have this knife in your set?"

- "How do you like that piece?"

- "How does that handle feel?"

- "Does that sound good?"

- Or my favorite, asked at a high point when the customer is clearly excited about something, "Can you see why everybody gets this stuff?"

Even a question as simple as "Right?" used at the end of a statement can be a powerful way to gain agreement. When used after a fairly logical statement, it becomes an irresistible force - the customer almost always says "yes" or nods in agreement.

Powerful, isn't it? Hey, that was a Positive Response Question, too, right?

Gotcha.

A Controlled Question is a question you can ask when you know exactly what the listener is going to say. But you ask because it gets them to tell you, rather than you telling them.

We've all heard the sales principle that "If you say it, it's hearsay, but if they say it, it's fact." Any sales situation can be DESIGNED to use lots of controlled questions.

Again, here are some examples from our Cutco training:

- "What can happen when you put a plastic handle next to a hot stove?"

- "What do you do with a serrated-edged knife when it won't cut anymore?"

- "After all, what's a knife supposed to do?"

"It melts." "Replace it." "Cut."

Everyone answers these questions correctly. That's why we ask them.

Again, it gets the customer to tell us a part of our sales presentation rather than us telling them everything. The more they are answering, agreeing, telling us what we want them to know, the closer we are getting to a sale.

I love when we promote Cutco's Forever Guarantee and then ask the prospect, "So why do you think our company can offer such a great guarantee?"

The customer generally responds, "Because it's a great product."

We've been there only a few minutes and barely shown them two items and they're already telling us the product is great. No wonder we sell well more than half of the appointments we conduct, usually with people who would not have considered buying knives that day had we not been referred to them.

Our sales presentation has been designed to incorporate dozens of quality questions that lead the interaction toward a sale. Of course, it helps having a legitimately great product to sell. But sales requires a lot more than just logic. Logic makes people think. But emotion makes people act.

Getting the customer involved in a dialogue with the sales rep reaches more of their emotions and makes them far more likely to buy.

## Dale Carnegie + Anthony Robbins = YOU (Wow!)

The last element of language I want to share in this chapter is what I've heard Anthony Robbins call "framing skills."

The basis of this idea is that the "frame" with which we choose to view our world affects the way we feel and everything we do is based on how we are feeling at that moment. Since how we are feeling is based on what we are focused on, we can learn to change people's behaviors by changing what they are focusing on. Framing skills help us do just that.

There are four framing skills essential to learn to become a powerful influencer:

1. The "As-If" frame
2. Preframing
3. Reframing
4. Deframing

## The "As-If" Frame

The essence of the "as-if" frame is to get someone into the frame of mind of having already decided to do something, for instance, having already decided to buy. There are key questions one can ask to get someone into that "as-if" frame of mind.

Here are some examples:

- "If you were to get a set of Cutco today, which one of these would you pick?"

- "If you did get this item, which investment plan would you use?"

- "If we found the exact house you were looking for, how soon would you want to move in?"

- "If we have a car that's just right for you, would you buy it or lease it?

- "If I could show you an investment you felt certain would benefit you, how much would you be prepared to invest right now?"

These questions put someone into the frame of mind of having *already decided to buy*. If they feel good in that frame of mind, you are well on your way to completing a sale.

You can also use this concept to help the people you work with start believing that a certain goal is possible. Rather than asking someone if they think they could accomplish something, ask something like this:

"If you knew that you were going to achieve your goal, how would it occur?"

By asking such an "as-if" question, you get the person to stop focusing on why something can't be done and instead focus on how it could be done.

A final application of the "as-if" frame is in motivating yourself. Any time you are considering a huge goal in your own life, try to get past the idea of whether the goal is possible and instead focus on how you are going to do it.

In 2000, I set a goal to create the first sales team to ever sell over $100,000 of Cutco in a single week, breaking the record of about $81,000. Rather than ever considering whether or not this was possible, I instead focused on creating a blueprint for how it WOULD happen.

Then I went about putting together the pieces of that blueprint. I was also able to promote the goal to my team with sincere confidence so that they believed it would happen and were thus more motivated.

We actually went well past $100k and sold over $114,000 in a week, paving the way for dozens of other Cutco sales teams to break that barrier in the years that followed.

We broke the previous record by over 40%!

What if you could do that in your business, next week or next year? Ask yourself, "How?" not "If?" and you just might find the answers.

## Preframing

The second framing skill is called preframing and this is probably my favorite.

The essence of preframing is to direct someone's focus in advance. I have a classic example from the Cutco business. Cutco knives are by far the world's finest, so as you might imagine, they also come with the world's finest price. Frequently I would have reps struggle early on, telling me that people aren't buying because the knives "are too expensive." Well, obviously, when I heard that, I knew that this rep himself thought the knives were too expensive. So, I would teach him to incorporate this phrase into the early stages of his presentations:

"Mrs. Customer, the first thing I want to tell you about Cutco is that it is absolutely not cheap. Now I bet you're actually glad to hear that, right? ... Because what happens with cheap things?" (Let Mrs. Customer answer here) "Exactly, cheap things are never good. Well, Cutco costs more than most other knives you could buy, but they are well worth it as you will see today."

Then the rep would move into showing the first item. Basically, this rep has taken something that could be a customer objection at the end and attempted to turn it into a positive benefit of the product instead. The genius of teaching this also lies in what effect this has on the sales rep.

If he says that to 10 customers, the customers each hear it once, but the rep hears it 10 times. So, gradually, he is becoming more convinced himself and building his conviction. By itself, that stronger conviction will lead to more sales because it will cause the rep to WANT to sell.

You can create preframes for many different kinds of objections. Another situation we would often preframe was when we would see a potential customer without her husband present. We would create a dialogue early in the presentation that would help cut down on the "I've gotta talk to my husband" excuse at the end.

Whether you are in a sales industry or just trying to influence people in a certain direction outside the sales field, you can think about the objections you commonly face and create ways of preframing those objections. Much of the process of parenting is preframing how you want your kids to react when they are confronted with certain situations or decisions in the future. When it comes to powerfully influencing people, preframing is a huge tool.

## Reframing

The third framing skill is reframing.

Reframing is basically about handling objections once you get them. It's important to realize two things about objections in sales. First, objections are normal. Very seldom will you close a sale without any objection, even when that person already intends to buy. Everyone wants to feel like they are getting a good deal and they will offer up objections sometimes just to test you.

Second, it's important to realize that objections are positive because they are actually a sign of at least some interest. If a salesperson in a store asked you to buy an item in which you had no interest whatsoever, you would not sit there discussing with them your concern about the size, fit, color, price, etc. You would simply say "no" and move on.

Therefore, an objection generally indicates that there is at least some interest, and thus, an opportunity for a sale. Every author in this book could probably write a whole book just on handling objections, so I'll keep this section very brief. Many sales books cover this topic in great detail.

For now, just remember the steps of the objection cycle:

1. Listen and pause before replying
2. Acknowledge the objection
3. Clarify what you think they mean
4. Offer a possible solution
5. Use questions to lead to the sale

When you sit back and listen intently to an objection (listening skills will be covered at length in my upcoming book), you give the feel of being truly interested in understanding how the other person feels. By pausing before replying, you give the other person a chance to expound and further clarifying how they are feeling.

The first thing out of your mouth should be an acknowledgement of the objection.

"I understand, Mrs. Customer, this is not a small decision we're talking about here."

"I know what you mean, Mr. Customer, $5000 for a watch is not cheap."

By acknowledging the objection, you are validating what the other person has said. You are deliberately taking a non-confrontational approach to handling the objection, putting yourself on their side of table, so to speak.

> *Every salesperson hears objections.*
>
> *The great ones are able to take the customers past that point of hesitation and into making a positive buying decision.*

This is infinitely more effective than arguing with them, trying to make yourself right or using confrontational words like "but." After this, you should clarify the objection in your words and check to see if you have fully understood the other person's position.

Then your job is to offer a possible solution to the objection. Possible solutions will vary greatly from one sales industry to another.

Good salespeople can work together to create viable solutions for most of the objections they encounter. After presenting a solution, you want to use a quality question to get a "yes" response and move the customer closer to the final "yes" indicative of a sale.

Reframing is probably the most challenging framing skill to develop, but clearly the one which pays the most dividends. Every salesperson hears objections. The great ones are able to take the customers past that point of hesitation and into making a positive buying decision.

That skill is what pays the big bucks in selling. After all, how much commission do you get for the sales that you ALMOST make? Zero.

Learn to use the skill of reframing to close a much higher percentage and your income can increase exponentially.

## Deframing

The final framing skill is called deframing. Deframing is about destroying someone's current focus and getting them to look completely in another direction.

You do this simply by changing the subject temporarily. Have you been on a sales call where it just didn't seem to be going anywhere? Maybe the other person was in a bad mood about something or just distracted. You will certainly leave without a sale if you persist on with them in that frame of mind.

So, this is a time to use deframing. By asking a completely unrelated question, you can turn their focus onto something else. Then you steer the conversation into some topic they feel positive about. After getting the other person into a renewed, more positive frame of mind, you can use a quality question to steer you back to the business at hand.

Sometimes, on a Cutco sales presentation, we run into a customer who seems totally distracted and just not into it. Continuing on in the same manner will surely result in a no-sale. This is a time for deframing.

After realizing she's in a stalemate that will lead nowhere, the sales rep can literally stop in mid-sentence and ask the customer an unrelated question like "What's that?" pointing to some interesting item on the wall.

The idea is to get the customer talking about something of interest to them, hopefully changing their focus temporarily and getting them into a more positive frame of mind.

The rep could then follow up with, "So what's the best purchase you've ever made?" and "Why?" Then, they can relate that back to Cutco and move back into the presentation with the customer (hopefully) in a different state than she was in before.

It doesn't always work, but you'd be surprised how often it does.

If you were selling investments and felt like you were running into a block in the conversation, you could change the subject by asking the customer something like, "So, where are you from originally?" and following up with "So, how did you reach the success you enjoy today?"

Getting the prospect to tell you a little about their story can often serve to change the mood and open them up more to what you are promoting.

"Wow, so you came to America with nothing and built a great life for yourself, huh? I have some great ideas on how you can ensure the same level of security for your children and grandchildren. Does that sound good?"

This line of questioning at least gives you a chance to regain the prospect's attention and interest, while persisting on in the face of a stalemate will surely lead you nowhere.

## You and I Can Change The World

Let me end where I began, with this statement: *Great influencers know what to say.* As you develop your language skills, the right words will come out of your mouth naturally. Precision language becomes a part of who you are.

Start with the basics:

- Make an effort to learn and use people's names.

- Offer compliments in a manner that conveys your sincerity.

- Frequently express your appreciation for other people.

- Make people around you feel important and be aware of building their self-image.

Then, gradually learn to use the advanced techniques of quality questions and framing skills to sharpen your influence. These skills can help you have a profound impact in your business and in your personal life.

I believe in the "ripple effect."

When a pebble is thrown into a pond, the ripple goes on and on until it reaches the other side of the pond. As you learn to more powerfully influence the world around you, you can have a positive impact on more people than you might think.

A Chinese general once said: "If the world is to be brought to order, my nation must first be changed. If my nation is to be changed, my hometown must be made over. If my hometown is to be re-ordered, my family must first be set right. If my family is to be regenerated, I myself must first be."

The same is true in reverse.

If we develop our skills in order to have a powerful impact in our family and our business circles, we can subsequently create a powerful, positive impact in our town, the nation and the world.

It all starts with you and me.

---

**Summary Points**

- Ask to know the name of the people you deal with, and call them by name during your interaction.

- State a compliment with sincerity, explain the reason for the compliment, and follow up with a relevant question.

- Based on the principle that high self-image leads to high performance, build confidence in those around you.

- Use quality questions to precisely guide your conversations.

- Influence others by creating a frame through which they hear or see your presentation.

- Handle objections by listening, acknowledging, clarifying, offering a solution, and using questions to ask for the sale.

- Your ability to influence the world around you will send ripples that will impact more people than you might imagine.

Carl graduated from Wabash College with a Bachelors Degree with a major in psychology and a minor in chemistry. He began selling Cutco Cutlery while in college. In personal sales, he set records for annual sales as well as 6 other national monthly records. Carl was inducted into the Cutco Hall of Fame and has owned and operated numerous small businesses including a taxi service and café in remote Alaska, an adventure guiding company, and an adventure film production company. Carl has traveled to more than 15 countries in search of adventure. He has climbed more than 50 mountains in his career including 20,320 foot Mount McKinley in Alaska, and 28,250 foot K2 in Pakistan. His most recent adventure was a 3500 mile bicycle trip across the United states from California to Boston. Carl currently works as an Inspirational Speaker, Adventurer, and Filmmaker and he serves as the Executive Director of LifeClimb.

# Learning the Ropes

## Carl Drew

## Story

"It's already happened twice today, Carl," I mutter to myself.

"You have to move faster. If you don't, you're sure to die. You can't stay here; you have to change ropes and keep descending. It's going to happen again. You have to move faster, Carl…faster!"

I'm alone, at 22,000 feet above sea level, hanging on a ½ inch thick rope with a near vertical 6,000 foot drop below me. My body wants to let go of the rope and collapse, but my brain does not want me to pay the price of failure. If I fall now, it won't just be the end of me, there will be no recognizable remains by which to identify my body. Should I fall, my body will go hurling down the mountain bouncing and flipping over the ice and rock galleys, before it reaches the base of the mountain.

To make matters worse, I'm hidden from the heat of the sun by the shade cast from 26,000-foot tall Broad Peak, the world's 12th tallest mountain. Broad Peak is located several miles to the southwest of the mountain I am descending, K2. At two degrees Fahrenheit, the moisture from my breath is freezing to the mask covering my face and icing up my goggles to the point that looking through them is pointless.

At this altitude the partial pressure of oxygen is so low that it does not permit the oxygen molecules in my lungs to bind strongly with my hemoglobin, which severely affects my body's ability to create heat and think clearly. It feels like it is fifty below zero and I'm thinking like a fifth grader.

But that's not the worst part.

The rocks hanging thousands of feet above me are not in the shade and they are being blasted by the radiant heat of the sun. The ice that has glued the rocks to the mountain for thousands of years is now melting. After breaking free, the rocks pick up speed and plummet down the face of the mountain at nearly 150 miles per hour.

"Carl, these rocks are quickly being heated by the sun," my logic tells me, "and if you don't switch ropes and get down off this mountain, the bigger ones will soon melt free of the ice. When they do, you will be smashed into pieces as they create an avalanche of rock and ice that tears down the face of the mountain destroying everything in its path. If you stay here you will certainly be dead. You must keep going. You must descend to Camp One, and then maybe you can rest there."

All of the sudden I hear a roar in the distance and it's getting louder!

It reminds me of the sound that can be heard in World War II films, when a pack of fighter planes dive in to bomb a city. Feeling certain there is not a pack of fighter plans in the sky, I reason it's the sound of hundreds of rocks free-falling through the air above me. A cliff of small boulders has just ripped loose thousands of feet above me on the mountain face. They are falling with such speed that I feel vibrations as one of them zooms past me. There is no doubt an entire cluster of rocks will be upon me within a matter of seconds.

Realizing I am fully exposed on the face of the mountain, my instincts take over as a sense of panic and doom sets in.

"What's the nearest point of safety? Where can I hide? There's nothing here to hide behind!"

Looking up and down the ice slope, I see my only chance of survival, a lone bolder, about one quarter the size of my body. It's poking out of the ice more than a football field away below me. It will be a miracle if I can make it there before these rocks obliterate my body.

"That's your only chance of survival," I tell myself.

"You've got to make it happen. Let go of the rope you're on, clip into the one beside it, and drop as fast as you can. I know this is going to be dangerous, but you're going to have to do it. Once you're clipped into the new rope, start rappelling and don't look back. You're probably going to lose complete control as you seemingly freefall, but just do it!"

## Changing Ropes

*"When you cannot make up your mind which of two evenly balanced courses of action you should take -- choose the bolder."*
- William Joseph Slim

As a child in the Midwest, I was destined to be a factory worker. As far back as I know, it was what the men in my family did for a living. I came from a long lineage of skilled tradesmen who worked with their hands. My grandfather built by hand the house he spent his life in, and the idea of calling a mechanic, plumber, or electrician to fix a problem around the house simply didn't occur. Those skills and ethics have traveled down generations in my family. If it was broken, we fixed it. If it needed to be built, we built it.

Growing up, love was bountiful in my family, but finances were not. We physically worked for money and we did it by working for someone else. It was the only way we knew to make a living, and working for someone else equaled security, safety and "a real job." Sometime around my middle school years, I realized this was a hard way to make a living. I concluded that the only way I was going to be able to help my family in times of need and have a few of the great conveniences of life, was to become a professional. Caring for people and having interest in the human physiology, I felt a career as a doctor would be the best choice.

From that point forward I focused on this goal.

I took all the medical related courses the high school offered and studied evenings and weekends to become an Emergency Medical Technician. I then went on to study pre-med at Wabash College in Indiana. During the summer following my sophomore year in college one of my pledge brothers, Dan, rang me to tell about his new summer job selling Cutco Cutlery. After telling me all about his new job, he asked about my summer employment plans. I told him I had just been offered a position at a local factory making $14 per hour and I was to be at work in two weeks.

Dan told me about his job and explained the concept of making a "commission." I was quick to challenge him and told him there was no way he would make the kind of money I was going to make working in the factory this summer. I told him to call me back when he made some "real money" and could back up his words.

Two weeks later Dan called me back and told me about his financial progress. I was impressed, but felt sales were not for me. I reasoned with him stating, "Kids like me need a secure job with an hourly wage so I can count on having the funds necessary to pay for school at the end of the summer."

Dan understood my line of thinking and the feeling of security I was seeking, but he was not ready to let me off the hook. He shared stories with me of all the fun he was having, the great education he was getting on life, the networking with people, the communication skills he was gaining, and best of all – the sales he was producing. He went on to share the freedom he had to plan out his own day and how enjoyable it was to spend time talking with people about an amazing product.

Dan encouraged me to start looking at other ways of making money so I would not be crushed by the same weight of financial stress that I had always experienced. He urged me to let go of the "rope of factory work" that my family had been holding onto for generations and fall into a new way of making a living.

Trusting Dan's advice and his concern for my well-being, I told him I would go and interview for a sales position. However, I was frightened inside because I knew I would not be able to attend school the following year if I didn't make enough to pay my tuition - Dan knew this as well. He knew it would be a big change for me and assured me that if I gave it my all, I would be able to "relax in style" at the end of the summer.

## Story

I unclip from the rope I was attached to and clip into a new one.

My body turns to face down the slope, my hands loosen my grip on the rope and I begin to drop down the face of the mountain. I begin running down the near vertical ice slope at a nearly uncontrollable speed. It feels awkward and is exactly the opposite of what feels natural to a climber, but at this point I don't care.

I'm in survival mode.

I don't take any time to look behind me. I know what is happening - the barrage of rocks is getting closer and closer by the second and I have a long way to go before I'll reach any semblance of safety. Jagged splinters of rock zing past me and I still have over one hundred feet left. One rock passes my head so close and fast, that I feel the vacuum it creates as it speeds through the air. I am constantly watching where I am going, while also watching what is coming from the opposite direction as it passes me at a much faster rate of speed.

## Working Hard

*"Do not wait; the time will never be "just right." Start where you stand,*
*and work with whatever tools you may have at your command, and better*
*tools will be found as you go along."*

- Napoleon Hill

I jumped into my demonstrations after my training course.

I remember the manager telling me that if I just got started and worked hard, that I would soon find I had all the skills and tools I needed to be very successful with the company. I also remember thinking to myself, if I worked hard enough, I could prove this "knife thing" was not for me and I could get on with my life.

I started calling everyone I could think of and set up demonstrations with them. I then fumbled my way through the presentations, dropping knives onto my prospects floors, tripping over my words, knocking over glasses of water on their tables, and even skipping pages of the prospectus just to get the demonstration over with.

Instead of handling objections, I would just agree with the prospect. The customer would say, "It looks like good stuff, but our knives are just fine." I didn't know that customer refusal was a natural part of the sales process. I would say, "Okay, well thank you."

With that, my book was closed and we moved onto other topics. This was okay by me. I wanted to get this thing over quickly. Besides, I was certain nobody was going to purchase my knives.

My manager, Jeff, seemed impressed when I showed up to the office two weeks later and told him I completed 80 appointments and demonstrations since training. He asked me to share my results. He was curious to see how my sales had gone, especially since I had skipped all the team meetings. I told him I had a whopping $2,500.00 in sales.

Jeff didn't share it with me that day, but I had smashed a national record for... the worst sales statistics in the history of the company!

I could not have done worse if I was selling mosquito nets at the South Pole. My meeting with Jeff was short and he concluded our conversation by encouraging me with stories of the successes others had. He told me their success was a result of hard work. He told me to consider myself blessed, because I had "hard work" down pat, considering the volume of demonstrations I had completed and that hard work was one of the most important ingredients in sales.

I left the office feeling somewhat relieved and encouraged that this "sales thing" had worked for others and that it would certainly work for me if I continued working hard.

## Story

"This is it, Carl. If you don't make this, you're done."

I push harder. My lungs fight to feed oxygen to my brain and my brain fights to make my muscles move faster. But it's no use. My lungs just can't get enough oxygen and I can't go any faster. In fact, I'm moving slower. It seems it is just too far to go. It's as if I have jumped into a swimming pool and begun running under water the entire length of the pool, only to discover that I still have to run under water all the way back to the other side of the pool.

The lack of oxygen is causing my chest to squeeze with pain and a massive headache begins to take on a life of its own. These are of little concern compared to the pain of not making it to that rock. That rock is my concern!

I keep telling myself, "Carl, you have to descend faster. Faster! Come on, faster man!" But, I can barely move. The lack of oxygen at this altitude is beyond belief.

## Having Belief and Faith

*"If you only do what you know you can do, you'll never do very much."*
- Tom Krause

The following day, Jeff and I sat down in his office for a consultation and he had me take him through my presentation.

I'm not certain what his thoughts were and he didn't share them with me at the time, but looking back I can imagine a few of the thoughts in his head were, "…You're fired…Your demo is dreadful… And maybe sales is not your thing." Jeff was a kind and wise manager and he refrained from squashing me like a bug. Instead, he shared the good news with me.

"You have an amazing work ethic and that is the main ingredient that brings one success. As a hard worker, you have the hard part out of the way, but there are two key ingredients that will take you to the top of your game in any aspect of life."

Curious to hear his advice, I leaned in closer to his desk and prompted him for the knowledge.

"Belief and faith," he told me.

"Belief in yourself and your product and faith in the process, tools and leadership you have to support you."

> *It's much better to ask yourself, 'how can I solve this problem' rather than focus on the problem.*
> *If you keep focusing on how this will not work for you, it won't.*
> *If you ask yourself how you can make this work, the answers will come.*

Jeff told me I needed to visualize myself actually making a sale and the customer being happy about having the product. He convinced me that both my belief and faith would be strengthened if I knew my sales demonstration from memory, if I started attending team meetings and absorbing the information like a sponge, and if I started looking at our competitor's products and pricing.

At the end of our conversation, he shared one last point.

"Carl, it's much better to ask yourself, "How can I solve this problem?" rather than focus on the problem. If you keep focusing on how this will not work for you, it won't. If you ask yourself how you can make this work, the answers will come."

I left the meeting and took Jeff's advice to heart. I realized that I had been focusing on how this "sales thing" would not work for me. This led to a lack of belief and faith in both the product and program, which in turn sabotaged my efforts and my sales. I decided it was time to commit to the program and figure out how to make this "sales thing" work for me.

Over the next week, I learned my approach inside and out, studied our competitors' products and price points, and continued meeting with prospects. It was now time to do some real knife selling.

## Story

I begin encouraging myself, "You've come too far to let it end here and you're capable of doing this. Think man! Think! How can you descend faster?"

Instead of focusing on the all the reasons I couldn't move any faster, I force myself to think of how I can overcome whatever is slowing me down. Within seconds, I realize the tension in the rope below me is preventing me from rappelling faster. I start flinging the rope below me in the air; this creates additional slack in the line and I begin to nearly free fall down the slope. Now, falling out of control, I'm approaching the outcropping rock with tremendous speed. I lock down on the rope, and it immediately breaks my fall.

Like Spiderman leaping from a building with his web attached to a pole protruding from a building in front of him, I fall in an arching motion and swoop down toward the rock. My body flips up right and slams into the ice with my face looking up toward the slope. There's a quick glimpse of the sky. It is grey with rocks that look like a swarm of vultures diving in to devour me. A quick roll to my left places me right under the rock. I lean my face onto the ice just under the rock.

"Yes," I mutter in an out-of-breath pant.

"I've made it."

But there is not much to be proud of.

I can only fit a small portion of my body under the protruding rock. With exploding force the rocks smash into my small shield. It feels like I'm the target in a shooting gallery and all I have to hide behind is a skinny telephone pole.

Hundreds of rocks are slamming into the ice all around me and I quickly notice that the position I'm in is leaving my knees and elbows exposed. I tuck into a fetal position and roll to put my pack between the falling rocks and me.

Whack! A rock cracks into my backpack piercing a gaping hole into it where my knee was just located. I pull my right elbow in, closer to my ribs.

Smash! Another rock smashes into the ice where my elbow was just located. I am fighting to survive not only the falling rocks, but also the lack of oxygen in my system. My heart is pounding with tremendous force and I gasp frantically for air. My mind quickly shifts to the rope that's holding me onto the mountain.

"Oh... I hope one of those falling rocks doesn't cut my rope."

Several minutes pass and the sound of falling rocks subsides as they bombard the cliffs below. I slowly recover from the adrenaline overdose and upright myself on the ice slope, where I begin wondering how much more of this I can handle.

I descend a few hundred more feet from my "shield rock" to the cliff that leads to the slopes that make up the final 4,000-foot drop to the base of K2. Several ropes pass over the cliff's edge. I choose the newer looking white and blue rope because it's the one my teammates fixed to the mountain only a few weeks ago. It should be strong and safe for a quick rappel down the cliff. I clip in and rappel over the edge.

As soon as I pass over the lip of the cliff, I notice something is very wrong. At this point I realize there is new danger.

"Crap Carl, this rope is cut. One of the falling rocks must have landed on it. You have to get off this rope now!"

But I can't.

## Accepting Risk

*"The winners in life think constantly in terms of I can, I will, and I am. Losers, on the other hand, concentrate their waking thoughts on what they should have done, or what they don't do."*

- Denis Waitley

I closed the first few appointments after that meeting with Jeff and it felt so good to see people buying my knives and enjoying them. Jeff was right - having faith in the process and believing in myself was the difference between success and failure.

But new problems crept in.

A few of my appointments cancelled and one of my orders had been returned. I was devastated and hurt by these setbacks and I approached Jeff to share my plight. Precious time and money that was to go to my college tuition had been lost. Jeff kindly listened and even let me cry without cutting me short.

A million thoughts began to swirl through my head. I explained to Jeff, maybe this was just not for me. Maybe I wasn't a natural salesman. What if I couldn't pay for college? What if all my orders were returned? What if I ran out of leads? The thoughts went on and on.

I told him how my friends laughed at me for being a knife salesman, that my father thought turning down a secure job with guaranteed pay was irresponsible and crazy and that perhaps, worst of all, I didn't like annoying people about buying knives.

When I was done, Jeff told me that all of these feelings are a natural defense system.

> ... *It is by risking nothing, that we risk everything.*

He let me know that his job was to help break my fall when these kinds of things happened, and that he was happy to act as a shield and absorb some of the impact. He explained that when we go beyond our comfort zone, our mind starts to make up all sorts of excuses as to why we should grip onto the old ropes of life.

"This is precisely why most people spend their entire lives doing something they dislike because they perceive it as being less risky than stepping out and living the life of their dreams." Continuing with this line of thinking, Jeff said, "Carl, it is by risking nothing, that we risk everything. Part of your problem may be that you have not yet accepted the idea that staying on your old familiar rope is the biggest risk of all. You need to let go of the idea that the rope you're currently hanging on is safe and rewarding, because compared to the other opportunities that surround you, it's not!"

## Story

I'm now hanging by the rope and my 50-pound backpack is pulling me backward. If I don't take control quickly, I'll soon be hanging upside down and unable to right myself.

"Quick, dig your crampons into the icy covered rocks," I think.

"Throw your axe into the ice above."

But it's a futile quest. My axe is stored on the back of my pack (which is standard procedure when rappelling), and my feet are flailing in the open air unable to kick into the ice.

"Get off this rope, it's not going to hold all this weight," I'm screaming inside. "Lord, let this rope hold. Please let it hold...just long enough for me to find one of these old ropes that might hold me."

I reach over my head and grasp onto an old rope left on the mountain by a climbing expedition that was there in years past. By holding onto this rope, I am able to again upright myself.

My eyes fixate on the stretched cut in the rope from which I'm hanging. I'm half amused by how on earth this rope is still holding me and half scared to death that it's not going to continue doing so. Although I still need to switch ropes while suspended in mid-air, I am forced to stop and catch my breath before I am able to regain enough strength to find another rope to grab.

## Learning from Leaders

*"Keep away from people who try to belittle your ambitions. Small people always do that, but the really great make you feel that you, too, can become great."*

- Mark Twain

Jeff suggested that to ease my transition into a new career, I should gain knowledge from those who are leaders in the industry. He explained that we could take huge short cuts in life and save ourselves a lot of pain if we could seek out and learn from those who already have experience and are successful in our area of study. As well, he pointed out the fallacy of asking just anyone for advice by saying, "Carl, you wouldn't ask someone who's always broke how to accumulate wealth, would you?"

Jeff suggested that I call one of my more successful colleagues and ask him what he's doing that has made him so successful. So I gave my pledge brother, Dan, a call and we talked for over an hour. He was becoming a great success in sales at Cutco, and he had a lot to teach me. I can't believe I didn't talk to him earlier about the lessons he had learned. He encouraged me, by sharing how he had dealt with many of the same obstacles and questions I had been struggling with. He told me that he was now doing well because he had solicited the advice of others who were much more experienced in the business than he was.

Dan was attending all of the sales conferences put on by his division and region. He saw them as an investment in his business, even though these seminars had some out-of-pocket costs. Dan explained that he was listening to sales programs and reading books daily that pertained to problems he was currently having in his life or business. He suggested that I take 30 minutes a day to read and educate myself on my business, as well as my hobbies. He said this would increase my ability to deal with situations that may unexpectedly arise.

I attended the next Regional Conference and I purchased my first audio book. From that point forward, I rarely used the radio in my car unless it was playing a tape or compact disk that educated me in some way.

I now had the skills I needed to begin rescuing myself. It was exciting!

## Story

Quickly I fumble to remove my gloves, being careful not to drop them. The cold air bites into my flesh, but it's do or die. The only choice is to switch over to the old brittle ropes and take the risk that they will hold together long enough for me to repair the rope where I'm currently dangling.

I pull a spare loop of rope from my harness, which my experienced climbing partner taught me to tie there for just such an occasion. Using this loop, I create a prussic knot around two of the old ropes, and I then clip it into my harness.

This primitive technique is now acting as a back up system for my high-tech ascender system that is attached to the cut rope. Pressed for time and fearing the falling rocks, I am torn between descending on the two old ropes and ascending the cliff to repair the cut rope. Knowing others may not have been as fortunate enough to escape this deathtrap, I commit to fixing the cut rope.

With frozen hands, I struggle to form a knot in the frozen rope, which is akin to braiding metal pipes together. Alternating hands, I thaw one hand and then the other hand by stuffing them into my down vest and placing them under my armpits. Eventually I knot the cut rope, and reconnect to it. As I begin my descent down this formerly cut rope, I thank the Lord for the lessons I have learned from those who are leaders in this field. This one technique may have just saved my life. I descend toward Camp One telling myself, "Man, I can't wait to get there...I can rest and wait out the rock falls; maybe brew some warm tea...I can continue my descent after the sun goes down...By then, the ice will refreeze and the rocks will stop falling." Unfortunately arrival at Camp One is a devastating sight as it comes into view. The tents are ripped to shreds.

For days, falling rocks had been bombarding the tents, blasting in one side and then out the other, taking cooking utensils, food, and sleeping supplies with them. The slopes below the tent look as if the fuel cells inside the tents have exploded turning our gear into shrapnel and launching it down the face of the glacier.

Heart broken and exhausted, I am overcome with feelings of disappointment, anger, frustration, and disbelief. I slam my climbing axe into the ice and collapse in the snow. My mind wanders back to those whose lives have been lost on this mountain and those forced to descend due to weather, injury or illness.

I begin to question what my fate will be on this mountain.

## Seeking Success

*"Those who turn back know only the ordeal, but they who persevere remember the adventure."*

- Milo L. Arnold

As the summer moved along, my closing ratio and average order size continued to increase by leaps and bounds. The more I knew, the harder I worked, the higher the weekly goals I set for myself became. After setting a few high goals and not reaching them and learning that a few representatives from my office had given up and moved on to another job, I began to doubt my abilities and my courage waned.

Once again, I started to question my decision to spend the summer working in sales.

I called Dan to get his insight into how I was feeling. Dan told me he had dealt with his own share of "falling rocks" that threatened to scare him off the climb towards his business goals for summer. He told of his own sales challenges of no-shows, cancelled appointments, and returned orders, as well as the number of times he had not hit the goals he set for himself. He told me stories of other representatives in his office who started out better off than he, but were no longer with the business.

> *Success is not measured by your sales, but by the obstacles you overcome while trying to succeed.*

He proposed that there were four main reasons for this: 1) they were afraid of working hard; 2) they didn't learn to have faith in the system and believe in themselves; 3) they couldn't let go of the perceived security of their hourly wage job; or 4) they failed to seek knowledge from leaders in the business.

"Other than that," Dan said, "Everyone is doing really well. You should be proud of yourself, Carl. You started out as one of the worst representatives in the country and have quickly risen to the top of the lists for weekly sales volume. We're making great money, buddy, and learning a lot about running a business and communicating with people. I look forward to seeing you at the last conference of the summer; it should be a great time."

I was very thankful for Dan's words and comments and it was of great comfort to know that I was not alone in this journey. Once again, I found Jeff was right in his advice to reach out and connect with those who were leaders in the business.

"Oh and Carl," Dan said, just before he hung up the phone, "don't get discouraged by what you see happening to other people or if you don't hit all your goals. Success is not measured by your sales, but by the obstacles you overcome while trying to succeed."

I decided that what Dan said made sense – there is no use in becoming discouraged by how I'm stacking up against others, whether I stack up better or worse. Even when things are going really well, you can make yourself feel pretty poor by focusing on how the best person is doing. And focusing on what's not going well only leads you to perform at a lower level and get discouraged.

It was time to take in the big picture of what the summer was all about and enjoy the ride to the end.

## Story

Retrieving my two-way radio from a pocket in my climbing suit, I call down to Base Camp to give them an update.

"Base Camp, this is Carl. I'm feeling good and strong. The tents in Camp One have been destroyed by rock fall. Much of the equipment is destroyed and the tents are torn. It is no longer safe to camp here. The rock fall is too dangerous."

The familiar voice of my expedition partner, Mick, responds back to me in his soothing Irish accent. "That'll be okay, just as long as yer safe. You're a brave lad for climbing to 26,000 feet."

I'm compelled to share my feelings of loneliness and impending doom with Mick.

"Mick, the sky is clear, but the amount of rock fall on the route is making the descent very dangerous. The falling rocks have nearly taken my life four times now and I'm scared of the descent from here to the base of the mountain 3,000 feet below me. This is the real 'death zone' on the mountain and it has me seriously concerned for my safety."

"Take your time," he tells me.

"Relax a bit and enjoy the scenery, you deserve it. We'll be right here on the radio if ya need anything. Give us a shout when yer good and ready to begin your descent."

Taking Mick's advice, I continue toward a rock pillar on the far side of the tents to seek protection from the rock fall. Removing my pack, I take out a water bottle and begin to drink. I know my body will need the extra energy for the final leg of the descent. As I consume liquid for hydration and Hammer Gel for energy, I can't help but take in the beauty of what I'm seeing.

I pause and look over the Karakoram mountain range. The silhouettes of the tallest mountains in the world form the horizon and the view stretches on forever. As far as the eye can see, it is only rocks, ice and snow. There is not a single sign of the existence of humanity or organic life, other than the tattered and torn climbing rope that disappears into a thin line below me and a few footprints in the icy snow in front of me.

It's just the mountain, K2, with a summit of 28,240 feet and me. It is unknown to most, but is rightly dubbed "The Savage Mountain" and is considered by many to be "The World's Most Difficult and Dangerous Mountain." Each year hundreds of people summit Mount Everest, but only a handful of climbers, if any, will be fortunate to reach the summit of K2. Statistically, the odds of returning from the climb alive holds even more devastating odds - for every four people who reach the summit, one dies trying.

For the moment, thoughts of getting off the mountain leave me. Instead, I am overcome with emotion. I can't help but contemplate all the impossible odds that had to be overcome for me to arrive at this point in my life. It hits me with magnificent force - I am living the dream that seemed nearly impossible 12 years ago and even more poignantly six months ago. I realize the value of this climb is not in how high I have climbed, but rather in the obstacles I had to overcome in the process of climbing the mountain.

"I can't believe I'm here," I hear myself say. "How did this happen? It was only six months ago that I declined this opportunity because it seemed completely impossible. I just could not see how everything could come together in such a short period of time."

> *I begin to realize that it is more painful to give up on the impossible dream and never know what could happen, than it is to chase the dream and face the risk of not achieving it.*

I begin to have flashbacks.

My memory jumps back to the moment when my long time climbing partner, Kurt, rings me on the phone about six months before the expedition would leave for Pakistan. He had taken the liberty of contacting the leader of the K2 expedition and had all but submitted an application for my acceptance without my knowing.

I remember Kurt prompting me to take advantage of this once in a lifetime opportunity. He felt I would greatly regret not taking on this adventure. I hear him telling me that if I didn't take advantage of this opportunity, I would look back at this moment in regret for the rest of my life. As Kurt continued talking to me, I began to think it is more painful to give up on the impossible dream and never know what could happen, than it is to chase the dream and face the risk of not achieving it.

It is with this understanding that I decided to reconsider my choices, depart from my old familiar rope and take on the risks that line the pathway of opportunity that leads to the climb of K2.

## Selling Hope

*"Since you cannot do good to all, you are to pay special attention to those who, by accidents of time, or place, or circumstance, are brought into closer connection with you."*

- St. Augustine

After a team meeting, I couldn't help but think of those representatives who had taken time out of their working hours to help coach myself and others by sharing what they had learned through their own experiences. By doing so, they not only gave us the tools we needed to succeed, but they helped to instill in us, the hope that we, too, could become skilled in sales like them.

As the weeks turned into months and my skill level grew, Jeff eventually asked me if I wouldn't mind talking to the newest representatives to share a few words of encouragement. I agreed, however, I was completely petrified of speaking in front of a group.

Jeff told me not to get too worried about the speech, as it would only be a minute or two, and then he explained to me one of the major driving forces in human spirit, hope.

"Hope," he said, "is what keeps us moving and growing as people, as a community and as a nation. When people lose hope, they lose a reason to keep growing and moving forward, and the moment we quit growing, we start dying. In the words of Benjamin Franklin, "Many people die at 25 and don't get buried until they are 75"; this is because they have lost hope. As we grow as leaders, it is our obligation to instill a sense of hope in those with whom we are fortunate enough to connect, and speaking is a great way to accomplish this. It's with this giving of hope that we are able to give to the world."

The following week, I shared with the representatives some of the lessons I'd learned over the previous months of sales. I shared the challenges and growth I had, the lessons others taught me which had helped me to become a better sales person, and I encouraged them that if they also followed the program and learned from the leaders, they would one day soon be at the top of the sales list.

I remember being completely petrified during my pep-talk. I couldn't think straight, my mind went blank, my legs were weak, my palms were sweaty, and I had a waterfall of sweat running out of my armpits. At the end of the speech, I wanted to slither out the door and disappear.

To my surprise, several representatives who were struggling came up to me and told me how valuable the information was to them. They shared that they were about to give up, and that my story and the challenges I dealt with were exactly the ones they were dealing with. It was then that I received one the greatest gifts of the summer; they said that the sharing of my experiences gave them the hope they needed to keep going on their new rope.

The following week those same representatives who were ready to give up showed up to the meeting excited to share their success. It was amazing to see what a few words of encouragement and guidance could do in changing someone's outlook and level of success.

As the summer came to a close, I realized the powerful opportunity I had been given to become one of the lucky ones who entered the sales field. It seemed that cutting myself free of my old familiar way of making a living, and taking a risk on this "sales thing" was the best decision I could have made.

I enjoyed the experience of selling Cutco Cutlery so much that I continued working for the company throughout my college years. Upon graduation, my uncle suggested that I consider forgoing medical school and continue following my passions for travel and sales. This came as quite a shock to me, because he, himself, was a family physician. His advice made sense to me and I continued working for Cutco.

Over the next 12 years, I used the experience, income, freedom, and time that sales provided me to live some of life's greatest adventures and to start several successful small businesses. Some of those adventures included traveling to 15 countries, a 21-day solo kayaking trip through the Florida Everglades, running 19 miles to the bottom of the Grand Canyon and then back out, competing in 15 half and full Ironman Triathlons, bicycling 3,500 miles across the United States from California to Boston, and climbing on more than 50 mountains - including the 20,320 foot high Mount McKinley in Alaska and the 28,250 foot K2 in Pakistan.

In the end, it ends up, cutting the old secure rope of an hourly wage, and ascending the challenging rope of sales, was the best risk I could have ever taken. It led me into a life of amazing adventures and opportunity. And although I nearly passed out when I was asked to speak to a room of 15 sales representatives, I have gone on to make a living as a corporate inspirational speaker and adventure guide.

## Story

Having taken time to relax, refuel, and reflect… I am ready to continue my descent.

I put on my pack, clip into the rope and lean back to begin my rappel to the base – 3,000 feet below. A few yards down the face I remember I was going to update Base Camp before I left Camp One.

I call Base Camp. "This is Carl. I'm going to leave Camp One and begin the final rappel to the base. I'm descending now; it is 9:11." Immediately that time makes me reflect about that date in history, I pause, and then add, "On second thought, I'm not superstitious, but being an American, something in me does not feel good about leaving when my watch says 9:11. I'm going to stay here for one more minute and leave when my watch says 9:12."

Then it happens. What I have feared all day long.

Craaaack!

A thundering sound rips through the mountain range, echoing off one mountain and then the next. It is a sound like I have never heard before from a falling rock. It is as if a major explosion took place on the mountain.

The communications person on the other side of the two-way radio is able to hear it come across the microphone.

"What was that?" I hear across the radio.

"I don't know," I respond. "But it sounds like really bad news. I'm in the ice gulley that the entire face above me funnels into!" My eyes widen and quickly scan the sky for falling rocks. But the sky is clear. Then my eyes come in contact with an astronomically huge boulder – the size of a school bus - thousands of feet directly above me. Even worse, it is hurdling through the air!

I cannot believe what my eyes are seeing. It is so huge that I first dismiss it as a slab of rock attached to the mountain. Then the gigantic boulder slams into the mountain with a thunderous roar - like a meteorite impacting the earth. It demolishes everything in its path and sends hundreds of rocks and huge chunks of ice catapulting into the air. An avalanche of huge rocks and ice is coming directly for me. The sky turns black with stone. No matter where I move on the rope, I am still fully exposed to the falling avalanche of rocks. My throat knots up as adrenalin begins rushing through my body. I take a deep gulp and my eyes widen. I realize I have no choice but to grab onto the rope with all my might and thrust my body into the ice and rock in front of me and hope for the best.

Clenching onto the rope, with my face buried in the snow and ice, I think to myself, "This is probably not the best way to spend the last few moments of your time on earth." In a moment of clarity, I realize that by gripping onto the rope I am limiting my choices and, more importantly, my chance of survival. Out of desperation, I unclip from the rope, which leaves me clinging to the side of the cliff without a rope to protect me from falling. In this moment of liberation , I'm now totally free of the restraint of the rope; in fact, a whole new world of possibilities has opened up to me. I am now able to seek protection in places where the rope would not permit me to reach.

I ascend as fast as I can to a boulder that is sticking out of the ice - just to the left of the climbing route. At the same moment, the avalanche of rocks crashes into the uphill side of the boulder, just as I reach the downhill side, which shields me from the falling rocks. Tucking in under the boulder, I find myself safely out of harm's way. Gasping for air, I struggle to survive the lack of oxygen in my system. A few minutes pass and the rock fall subsides. I take a few moments to catch my breath and plan out the final part of my descent.

As I gaze over towards the route, I begin to burst out in tears of laughter and joy. It dawns on me, that the rope I had felt protected me from so much risk was the biggest risk of all. It had been severed in half by the falling rocks.

I hear the words of my Cutco Manager, Jeff, in my head on my descent to Base Camp.

"Part of your problem may be that you have not yet accepted the idea that staying on your old familiar rope is the biggest risk of all."

This makes me burst into laughter as I imagine myself responding to Jeff's wisdom by saying, "Yep Jeff, you're right... my old familiar rope is the biggest risk of all. Do you know where I can find a sharp knife to cut the rope with?"

---

### Summary Points

- Have belief in yourself and your product, as well as in the process of selling.

- If we focus on why something won't work, it won't. When we ask ourselves how to make something work, we will find a way.

- Success is measured by the obstacles that you overcome while trying to succeed.

- Life can be a wonderful adventure if you are willing to risk a little.

- It is more painful to give up on an impossible dream and never know what could happen, than it is to chase the dream and face the risk of not achieving it.

- A few words or encouragement can go a long way in changing someone's outlook and ability to succeed.

- Whatever we can do to help one another succeed in our personal dreams and business goals is the best gift we can give to each other.

Starting as a sales rep in 1988, J Brad Britton finished his career with CUTCO as Western Region Manager in 2005, amassing over $220 million in career sales, leading his team to six national championships in seven years, including an unprecedented four in a row. Having developed hundreds of the company's top leaders in sales and management, J Brad's passion for development of top sales leaders pioneered several company programs and led to the creation of the CUTCO Sales Professional position. He is currently a network marketing professional and is launching a direct sales division for five major publishing companies.

# When Is It Best to Give Up?

## Brad Britton

For centuries, it has been used to teach valuable lessons to sales people, teachers, pastors, children and others. Motivational speakers love to tell it and use various interpretations to inspire audiences. It has been referred to so often that many people may believe it has been overused and even lost its effectiveness with experienced sales people and managers.

It is "The Parable of the Sower."

If you are a person who thinks you know the story from top to bottom and think you have a deep understanding of all the interpretations and implications of the story, then this chapter is for you. On the other hand, if you have very little experience studying or being taught the story, then this chapter may be even more suited for you!

Let's start with the basics. This is the stuff you probably already know. The story, in the New Britton Paraphrased and Expanded Version, goes like this:

There was this farmer who had this big basket of good seeds. This farmer - we will call him Fred - being an industrious fellow, decided that rather than grinding up the seeds and making flour for bread or some other kind of cooking, he would plant his seeds. Fred did this, so that next season he could grow a large crop and have way more seeds than he did in the first place.

Now, Fred is not exactly the most skilled farmer in the land. He just doesn't have a whole lot of experience planting seeds, but he understands the basic concept – throw the seeds out there, let the sun and the rain do their thing and then the seeds will grow into plants. At some point in the future, these plants will need to be harvested and so, Fred knows that there will be more work to do later when it comes to picking, sorting and cleaning.

Alas, Fred is pretty smart and he knows that he will never even get to the picking and other stuff, unless he gets the seeds planted in the first place. He could sit back and dream all day about how full his harvest will be, but dreaming without action is just wishful thinking. So out he goes to sow his seeds with nothing more than a basic plan.

When he cast his seeds onto the ground, some of the seeds landed on a path that was very hard and beat down from all the foot traffic that came and went. The ground was pretty hard; in fact it was too hard for the seeds to take hold, so they ended up just sitting there until eventually some birds flew down and ate the seeds. Since there has never been, to my knowledge, a devoured seed that has grown into a plant inside the stomach of a living animal, those seeds are pretty much not going to produce anything to harvest.

But not all the seeds fell on the path. Some of the seeds actually fell on ground that allowed them to take hold and start to grow. Now, just because a seed starts to grow into a plant, does not mean the plant will reach its full potential.

For example, if the soil is not very deep or is full of rocks and gravel, there is a good chance the roots will not fully develop. This is what happened to some of Fred's seeds. As soon as a few hot days came along, the fledgling plants got all dried out and pretty soon they died altogether. It is a sad, but common thing that happens with seeds that fall on the shallow or rocky soil. (It is even worse when the soil is shallow and rocky.)

> *If we want more abundant life, we have to give up the life we currently have.*

So far, Fred's big plan does not seem to be going so well. But do not fret for Fred because he knew that this kind of thing might happen, which is why he spread out lots of seeds in all kinds of places. He knew that other people had been successful at this sowing and reaping thing before, so he just figured he would learn from other people's experience and learn from his own experience. After all, learning from every experience minimizes failure.

Keep in mind that Fred didn't even know yet that the birds ate some of his seeds and he didn't know that some of his seeds were going to start to grow and get all dried out. He was only in the sowing phase of this whole process. He didn't just throw out one seed and watch to see what happened for the next few weeks. He was keenly focused on getting the seeds out there and he knew he could learn more about the harvest season after he got the seed planting done.

As he kept on sowing, some of Fred's seeds fell onto soil that was not rocky or even shallow. These seeds took hold and started forming roots and things seemed promising for a while, but eventually, a bunch of weeds and thorns started growing alongside Fred's plants. These weeds and thorns eventually cut off much of the sun, soaked up much of the rain and soon the roots of the good plants and the weeds and the thorns got all mixed up. This caused Fred's plants to be very weak. Many of the good plants died and the ones that survived were barely worth anything - not even really worth the time to pick, sort and clean.

Now if Fred had been a more experienced farmer or maybe if he had just been paying better attention to these seeds, he could have gotten his hands a little dirty and plucked out all those weeds and thorns. It might not have been the most glamorous or fun part of creating a bigger harvest, but it sure could have saved some of those plants that were affected by the weeds.

But in Fred's defense, if nobody took the time to explain to him the importance of checking in on those seeds every day, how could he be expected to know that he should be constantly working to protect and foster those little plants? I suppose he could have picked up a book at the library or even asked a more experienced, successful farmer, but maybe he just didn't think of that.

Actually, he was probably busy learning what to do when harvest season came. Next time around, he will have more experience and more time to care for more of the plants that start to grow.

The best part of the story, for Fred and his family at least, is that some of the seeds fell on very fertile soil. No rocks. No weeds. No birds. No thorns. Everything happened just right and the seeds took root, the roots spread and the plants grew.

When the harvest came, some of the seeds had produced plants that multiplied the original seed 30 fold. Some of the seeds multiplied 60 fold and some multiplied 100 fold. Wow!

OK, so that's the story. I hope you like the paraphrased and expanded version. Giving the sower a name seems to bring the story to life a little more, don't you think? The most common interpretations tend to focus on Fred's actions, on the four different terrains or even on the harvest.

Let's face it, Fred is destined to succeed for several reasons: He had a good basic plan. He got started, even though he didn't know everything. He focused on the task at hand. He was persistent. He was not afraid of hard work. He didn't get distracted and he knew he had more to learn.

We can also learn from a big mistake Fred seemingly made. He didn't ask for help. Chances are, if he had sought some counsel, he may have not wasted so many seeds on all the bad soil. It might have been worth Fred's time to find a good partner or two to help with the weeds and thorns.

"It's better to have a partner than go it alone. Share the work; share the wealth." Ecclesiastes 4:9

We can learn great lessons by focusing on the soils. Looking inward, we can discuss which kind of soil is in each of us. Looking outward, we can realize that not everyone will receive our message the same way we see it. We can learn that good qualifying of prospects would be like finding the fertile soil and planting only there. The soils can certainly tell us much.

What about the harvest? It is no coincidence that the different plants produced different quantities at the harvest; some produced 30 fold and some produced 100 fold. Some customers or sales people produce a great deal more than others, but all that produce have value. Putting in exactly the same amount of effort with one person could produce two or three times the results with another person.

Learning the harvest lessons can add greatly to our wisdom.

---

*There is so much irony in the excuse that so many of us mistakenly throw around as if it were really true: "I don't have the time to do ..." This may be one of the worst possible things we can think and say.*

---

So what is new about all this? Not much yet, but here comes the least talked about part of the story.

In the first few sentences, we learn that Fred The Sower had some seeds. The best part about this whole thing is what he chose to do with the seeds. He gave them up!

What if Fred had thought about all the risk associated with throwing those seeds all over creation? What if he had decided to make bread and feed his family today? They may have been hungry! What if Fred had hoarded his seeds? Or only planted a few of them? Fred could have chosen to do a number of other things with those seeds, but he chose to sow them.

Wow! This is huge!

The significance of that decision can teach us more than everything else in the whole story. Here is the principle: *we have to give up that which we want*. This is a very prevalent theme in many theologies. If we want more abundant life, we have to give up the life we currently have.

Have you heard the phrase, "to die is gain?" If we want money, we need to give up the money that we have – plant it. If we want more free time, we have to give up the free time we have now – plant it. We have to use (invest) that time to gain skills, meet prospects, work our business, share our product or service, place advertising, doing whatever we can do to free up more time in the future.

Often, a person can invest as little as an hour a day for a few years and have that small daily investment pay off handsomely - 30 fold, 60 fold or even 100 fold. There is so much irony in the excuse that so many of us mistakenly throw around as if it were really true:

"I don't have the time to do …"

This may be one of the worst possible things we can think and say.

> *Empowerment comes from the knowledge that we are not victims of circumstance.*

Every human being is equal in two important ways – in the eyes of God and in how much time we have in a day. We all have 24 hours in a day – 168 hours in a week. We each choose exactly how we use that time. To say that, "I did not have the time," to do something is virtually never the truth.

It is much more accurate to say, "I chose to do something else."

An important point to make is that it is okay to choose whatever you want. Just don't say that you "didn't have time" to read that book or attend that meeting or call that prospect because you had something else you chose to do.

Tell the truth (mainly to yourself).

If you have a day planned with your family on Saturday and your boss asks you to work that day – you have a choice to make. Whichever you choose is fine. Just don't tell the other party that you "do not have time."

The most important person to be honest with is you. If we can come to grips with the fact that our life is a result of the choices we have made and our future is a result of the choices we are making, we will almost automatically begin making better choices.

Empowerment comes from the knowledge that we are not victims of circumstance. We have choices to make every day. We can feel trapped due to certain circumstances and feel like we have no choice in certain matters, but we do always have a choice. There may be only one choice that we feel like we can live with and that is the proof that we are making the choice.

There is an old saying, "You can pay me now or you can pay me later."

You may have also heard, "The pain of discipline weighs ounces, while the pain of regret weighs tons."

So many times we make small, seemingly insignificant choices each day that either move us closer to our hopes and dreams or farther away.

Consider this sad truth: Most people give up what they really want for what they can have right now. This is the story of Esau (see Genesis 25:29-34). Fred the Sower teaches us the exact opposite – give up what we can have right now for what we really want.

You reap what you sow. It really is that simple.

So what do we do with this newfound wisdom? Here is a three-step action plan:

1. Start by paying attention to the reasons (excuses) you give for doing or not doing things. Avoid saying, "I don't have time," or "I didn't have time." Instead, think about the choice that is being made and make sure it is really the choice you want to make.

2. Consider what you really want and what you will have to give up. Develop an understanding of the principle of sowing and reaping. Make sure what you want is well worth what you are giving up. Dream big. Your dream should have at least the value of more than 100 times what you plant.

3. Finally, get help. When determining your basic plan, it is a good idea to get some outside input, preferably from someone with more experience than you have. If there is no one with more experience available, get input from a positive, encouraging source that wants you to succeed. Also get help with the work itself. Scripture states that if one can put a thousand to flight, then two can put ten thousand to flight. This defies basic mathematics, but it holds very true. Be selective when searching, but find a partner to share the burden and to share the rewards. Do this and you will accomplish exponentially more than you ever could alone.

After all is said and done, what do you want? In other words, what are you willing to give up?

---

## Summary Points

- If we want a more abundant life, we have to give up the life we already have.
- We can avoid wasting time by getting help from others.
- Finding qualified prospects is like finding fertile soil and planting where it counts most.
- We have to give up that which we want.

- Saying "I choose to do something else" is more accurate than saying "I don't have enough time."

- Empowerment comes from the knowledge that we are not victims of circumstance.

- Most people give up what they really want for what they can have right now.

John Ruhlin is the number one all-time sales representative for Cutco Cutlery. He found his way to the top by pioneering a corporate selling program starting at the age of 22. In addition to making a difference in the Cutco world, John is also well known for his unrivaled ability to network with movers and shakers. John uses his networking connections to support over six different charities around the world. John is a member of Entrepreneur's Organization, a board member for the Front Row Foundation, as well as Life Climb.

# The Three Currencies of Life
# How to Go from No One to #1!

## John Ruhlin

Thinking back to my youth, I still remember the long summer days I spent on my grandpa's pontoon boat and the lessons I learned there.

It's not exactly the place where you would expect a world-class business-lesson to take place between a grandfather and pre-teen grandson, but that was my first real-world classroom.

Since my immediate family did not come from money, our resort destination of choice (or lack there of) was my grandpa's house, 20 minutes away. It was there that I spent much of my childhood summers doing what I loved more than anything in the world: fishing.

I spent hours on that boat and most of the time was spent in silence waiting for my bobber to sink below the surface. Periodically, my grandpa would break the silence with a story. Most of the time his stories related to auctions or something involving a unique business deal he was involved in, while he created from scratch the largest auction company in Ohio.

I do not remember most of the wisdom my grandpa shared with me, but for some reason a question he asked me when I was 11 years old is burned into my mind: "Which would you rather have John, one million dollars or a penny that you could double every day for a month?"

I remember answering quickly and confidently and thinking what a dumb question.

"The million dollars, of course!"

From the scowl on my grandpa's face it did not take me long to realize my obvious calculation was somehow wrong. I remember thinking, "How could that possibly be? There is no way a penny doubled 30 times could equal anywhere close to a million dollars."

"You could have had over 3 million dollars if you had started with the penny," my grandpa smirked, "You see Johnny, if you can learn how to invest a penny and then sell it for two pennies, you will always have the ability to make an infinite amount of money and you won't be trading time for money."

He had my attention. Grandpa continued.

"People that work for others trade time for money, however, when you trade money for money, you are in control of your time and your opportunity is limitless. If you can take that concept and do it 30 times in a lifetime, you will never want for money. Start with one and double it 30 times."

I remember thinking, "This doesn't sound like a hard thing to do."

Looking back I now call that lesson my "rich dad" moment. It was when the entrepreneurial bug first bit me and my mind realized a new way of looking at the world.

Throughout the history of selling, fishing has been used as an analogy. You probably have heard most of them if you have been in sales for even a short time, sayings like, "You gotta cast where the fish are" or "You have to use the right bait" or my favorite, "Cast enough times and you will catch the fish."

These analogies go back further than most people realize, with the bible being the first reference. Jesus called out Peter and John saying, "I will make you salesmen" or in his terms, "fishers of men." The relation between fishing and sales really is a great analogy for many reasons. Most people can relate to the frustrations of fishing for hours and not catching anything while the person beside you can't reel them in fast enough.

When this happens, we think to ourselves, "What could they possibly be doing that is so different? I mean for crying out loud, they are on the same boat as me, with basically the same lures and fishing for the same amount of time. Why are they catching fish and I am not??!!"

Your beliefs have a huge impact on you. Beliefs like - you have to come from the right family or have a certain amount of money or have a certain position within the company. I will also share my experiences of proving these and a number of other myths wrong, but for now, I want to share a few other experiences in becoming the number one sales rep of all time in the 59 year history of Cutco.

I don't say that boastfully, but to bring credibility that what I have to share is of some value for those out there aspiring to create sales for themselves or their teams. I will tell you that as I go into my 8th year with Cutco, I have just realized that my education began long before my time with Cutco and continues to this day to show me how much I have to learn about the craft of selling.

It is ironic for me that my first lesson about business and sales came from none other than my summers with my grandpa fishing.

Even at my young age, I had pennies.

And with pennies I could start my career as a sales person. It didn't take long for me to want to try this out. My first venture started down a familiar and favorite road of mine…candy. I remember walking into the local corner store in our town of less than a 1,000 looking for my first investment. It didn't take me long to settle on a personal favorite: sweet and yet, so sour, little yellow spheres or as most people know them - lemonheads.

I told my mom I was buying the whole box and was really excited to hear the cost had dropped from 15 cents to 10 cents. My cost per box: 10 cents. I was selling them for 25 cents at school during recess.

The following year I was in middle school and graduated to buying blow pops for 15 cents and selling them in study hall for 50 cents. My grandpa was right...buy it, double it, sell it. Trading money for time. There was no limit to how much money I could make when I applied this principle because I wasn't trading time for money. I was doing the exact opposite.

That lesson has served me well as I have continued down my business journey. What my grandpa never had the opportunity to share was that there were other currencies to be leveraged. Money was definitely one of them, but it was not by far the most powerful. During the 8 years of selling Cutco, I have experienced and been shown first hand the power of using three other currencies to create a type of wealth that goes beyond the monetary.

Below I will share with you the powerful currencies of Time, Talent, and Treasure. I will share with you how these three principle currencies can be used to create an amazing life for yourself and others.

By focusing on the benefits to others, we are most equipped to realize our personal bests.

## The First of the "Three Currencies" is Time.

I would like to ask you a question - time is what?

If you're like most business people you probably answered, "Time is money."

Time is the first and most difficult of all the currency principles available to you. I share this one with you first because, although it's the most challenging currency to spend on others, it holds the greatest of rewards life has to offer you.

I'm sure you would agree that it is easier to write a check, than it is to take the time to become physically involved. Many of my cherished relationships have resulted from taking the time to join in.

As Woody Allen has so famously said, "I showed up."

I said "yes." I found a way to be there with all of life's hectic schedules around me.

Being able to say "yes" is one of the most powerful privileges of being an independent contractor or a sales representative. It is unfortunate, however, that most people do not take advantage of this opportunity. The majority of people working 9-5 cannot say "yes" like a person who controls their own schedule.

> *It is the case that the business people who are operating at their highest potential are also people who realize there is more to life than what money can provide.*
> *They are people who understand that there is more to life than business development.*

In sales, it's easy to justify taking time to go to a networking event or two or to attend a seminar or a benefit dinner. This is easier because it feels good and makes sense according to the standard business model - you are investing your time to be a "networker" and create new business connections.

But the question I would like you to ask yourself is, "Who are you connecting with?"

In most cases, you are connecting to people like yourself. You are connecting to other small business owners and starving sales representatives who are looking for their next deal, which of course is not a bad thing. If you're like I was, you are justifying this expenditure of time with the couple business deals you get every now and again.

When I broke down my personal time spent in this way, down to income per hour, I realized a couple different things.

One, I would have been better off taking extra time to further develop the relationship with my current customers. I could redirect this same time in a much more profitable way by continuing to build a stronger relationship with them, servicing them at a higher level and getting leads from them. This not only made more financial sense, but it gave me the satisfaction of knowing that I was truly servicing my customers at a high level.

Two, through servicing my customers at this level and developing deeper relationships, I began to have 'quality conversations' about life and their perspective on service. It is the case that the business people who are operating at their highest potential are also people who realize there is more to life than what money can provide. They are people who understand that there is more to life than business development.

As a result, they are volunteering their time to serve others.

> *He could have easily cut a check to either cause and been off to his next business deal because his time was worth too much to be spending time serving, but that is where you will find the best leaders - out there serving with their time. They are investing in people, not just their own pocket book.*

Going further with this concept of service, I began to realize the important duty I have to go beyond the bottom line and give my time to those who need it the most. If you are looking to take a quantum leap in your business and the development of yourself, you may need to take a new approach, as I did.

I remember sitting down a few years ago with Jim Karman, the former president and owner of RPM. Over the last 30 years he and his partner built the company from seven million to two billion. Here sat a man who had incredible wealth and connections all over the country. Almost anything he wanted was at his finger tips. If I had not been introduced by his sons, you know where I would have had to go to cross paths and spend time with him.

Country club? Nope.

Networking event? Not even close.

He was spending most of his time in West Palm Beach volunteering at the police department and at the local cancer center. He was giving back and loving every minute of it. He could have easily cut a check to either cause and been off to his next business deal because his time was worth too much to be spending time serving, but that is where you will find the best leaders - out there serving with their time. They are investing in people, not just their own pocket book.

My feeling has always been, I make enough mistakes on my own, if I can model successful people and glean their wisdom to avoid a few mistakes, I will be way better off.

> *If you want to rub elbows with the world's elite, take a pass on the country club golf game and start showing up at the soup kitchens and prisons.*

Taking the time to serve accomplishes a number of things.

First, you gain perspective on just how blessed you are. When we realize what real day-to-day struggles really are, stresses just melt away. Many times the people we are serving end up teaching us more than we teach them.

Second, there is also something magical that takes place in the human soul when you serve one another - our ability to love increases when we take the time to love others.

And third, if you want to be around the type of people that could take your business to another level, you will often find them serving and getting their hands dirty. There is no substitute for the bond created in serving along side one another…the ties and titles come off and it's just people serving their fellow man.

At a core level we all want our lives to have mattered and once most people climb the ladder of financial success, they realize that writing checks just won't cut it. If you want to rub elbows with the world's elite, take a pass on the country club golf game and start showing up at the soup kitchens and prisons.

So, I'd like to ask you that question again…Time is what?

Time is power, the power to impact the lives of others and the quality of life you are now living. As sales people and business owners, we have the ability to leverage the power of time.

If you serve with your currency of time, you will take your life and business to a new great level. You will not only learn more about yourself in those few hours, you will meet the men and women who have figured out that life is not about getting another dollar, nor giving another dollar, but serving one another with another hour.

I challenge you to spend this currency in a way that will have greater impact on the lives of others in a way that money just can not do.

## The Second of the "Three Currencies" is Talent.

Ask almost any salesperson, business owner or network marketer if there is anything they enjoy more than a referral or someone helping them get connected to a potential A list client and most will answer "no."

Connecting talented people with other talented people multiplies the respect every person that touches those two people has for you. Your name starts coming up in conversations with strangers and more strangers, something a million dollars of advertising could never buy.

Referrals and connections are like pure oxygen for someone in business. With the amount of distractions and directions people are being pulled in combined with the increased speed of business, a phone call from a trusted friend or business associate is still the most efficient and effective way to cut through the madness and make things happen.

If everyone loves being connected, why do so few people go out of their way to connect to others? Too busy, some say. Others say their contacts are too important to share with others. While still others think they don't really have access to a network of people to tap into.

A perfect example of this just occurred a year ago. A friend that I meet with on a regular basis, Daniel Moneypenny, has a branding company and an incredible network. We often sit down for breakfast at the local Bob Evans once every couple of months to discuss ideas and potential contacts with one another.

> *The best compliment you can give a sales person or a business person is a referral or connection.*

When I came home from a particular meeting with a very connected gentleman named Peter Strople, I knew I had a decision to make.

Peter was beyond connected, with a rolodex containing over 9,000 names of some of the most influential people in the world of business. I knew Daniel would love to connect with a guy so connected to so many influential people, but inside there were selfish thoughts ringing in my head.

"This contact was so great," I kept thinking.

"Do I really want to share his contacts with others? If they connect, they will do all these great deals together and I will be left in the dust."

I shook off the thought, trusting only good things would happen if I made the effort to connect them. It did not happen immediately, but six months after that meeting I was invited by Daniel to attend a meeting Peter was attending to meet with some of Daniel's top connections.

The connection of Peter and Daniel that day multiplied into four other high level contacts and an invite into an exclusive group of high level entrepreneurs called EO.

The ripple effect of this one decision is continuing to bring forth new and exciting business opportunities that would have never occurred had I not gone out of my way to connect talent with talent. That is the beauty of this concept. It is not incremental, but exponential growth.

And the best part is - it is really enjoyable.

Ask yourself, "What contacts do I have that others could benefit from? How can I start spending my currency of "talented contacts' in a way that will benefit others?"

Spend this currency wildly and widely and you will build yourself a respect from others that is unmatched by any other compliment you could give to those with whom you come in contact.

The best compliment you can give a sales person or a business person is a referral or connection.

Start spending this currency today!

## The Third of the "Three Currencies" is Treasure

I can still remember the moment. It was December 25,1986.

I was 6 years old and dressed in my PJs with the footies attached. I woke up an hour before my parents and crept slowly down the stairs. I started rummaging through the gifts Santa stashed under the long needle pine tree that kept poking me with its dry needles every time I reached under it to inspect another gift.

I remember wanting so badly to pick up a box that was just the right size and weight. A size and weight that would tell me I got the gift of my dreams - a Thundercats race track.

There was no mistaking the expression on my face when I picked up the final and last gift under the tree. It was the expression of sheer delight and joy. I could not have been a happier boy that day.

In fact, the excitement of that gift still makes my hair stand with joy today. What a memory!

For some reason as we grow older our concept of gifting changes.

Maybe it's because we no longer have to wait to get those special gifts from others because we just go out and buy what we want when we need something. Or maybe it's because we only give gifts that we have already specified into our holiday giving routine. Deep down though, almost everyone I have come across still loves getting surprised with a gift.

When is the last time you received a gift that was truly given with your taste in mind?

> *A gift in my mind is not meant to create an action, but to solidify in their mind who you are, so that when you cross paths with them again, there is strong rooted feeling and memory associated with you.*

For most, I would venture to say that it was probably an anniversary, Valentine's Day or some distant memory from when you were a child. The great value that lies in the currency of treasure, is that you have the ability to re-ignite the great sensations within the lives of your business contacts with the memory and delight that comes with a well-chosen gift that is unexpected and has no strings attached.

A gift in my mind is not meant to create an action, but to solidify in their mind who you are, so that when you cross paths with them again, there is strong rooted feeling and memory associated with you. They will want to take your call and make time for you. They go the extra mile to listen to what you have to offer or say and often times they may not even remember why they feel so drawn to your ideas.

Think about a typical office setting. When the mail comes into the office, most of us get a stack of white envelopes and the majority of them are bills. Maybe every once in a while a letter or handwritten note comes in the mail and it is the first thing we open, that is, unless there is a box.

That box, no matter the size, rises to the top of the pile and gets all of our attention. We want to know who sent us something and more over, what is in that box. Whether it is a result of Christmas pasts or of how God wired us, that box has our fullest attention.

Now unfortunately most people are disappointed when they open the box because they are longing to be surprised with that special gift.

In reality, most gifts that are sent are neither special nor impressive. They are token gifts like gift baskets or cheap desk items, which more often than not, leave the recipient feeling a bit more depressed than if they had received nothing at all.

Every once in a while someone comes through with a gift that exceeds our expectations and we are like children.

A smile comes over our face and we can't wait to try it out, play with it and show off our new item! We invest so much time, effort and money on things like networking and tradeshows to get in front of people, but often the ball is dropped when it comes to solidifying the relationship and standing out.

If we do this, our time is not invested, it is spent.

And having been spent, it is wasted. What people do not realize is that there are hundreds of people vying for your contacts' attention. As soon as you are no longer with your new contact, their minds are being occupied with a hundred other people saying and asking for the same things.

There are two ways to combat this potential loss - never leave the person's side or leave them with something that they will never want to leave their side.

> *Compliments are appreciated and hand written notes are remembered, but well-chosen gifts are talked about with others and never forgotten.*

I remember a chance meeting I had with a top Nike executive at the Final Four event in Atlanta in April of 2007. We really hit it off and ended up spending the evening together at a local hangout. We even spent time grabbing a meal at a popular diner at 2 a.m..

Now, most would consider this a pretty memorable moment and an easy relationship to continue after the event. But this was not so.

After that event, I tried to follow up and stay in touch with this person and I did not have much success.

I remember thinking, "She is busy taking care of business, so why would she take my call?"

Remembering she was a trainer at one point in her life, I knew she was into health and taking care of herself with home prepared meals. So, I sent her Cutco personalized knives with both her name and the Nike logo engraved on the blade of the product. Within a few days I got the call I had been wanting to receive for months.

Several months passed and I found myself wanting to set up a meeting with her at the Nike headquarters in Portland. Once again, I needed to break through the clutter of her business schedule and get her attention. Having made notes in my business rolodex after the Final Four event, I noted that she was a California Golden Bears grad (keeping track of conversations is a must in high level selling).

It just so happened that I was working on a project that involved making exquisite wood carvings with NCAA team logos carved into them. I made up one with the Cal logo, shipped it off to the Nike Headquarters and waited for the call.

Wow, did I get it!

The voicemail she left was so overwhelming that, to this day, I still have it saved and listen to it from time to time when I need a reminder of the importance of the currency of treasure or a motivational moment in my day. Not only did I get the meeting amongst an impossible schedule, but she took the time to give me a personal tour of the Nike campus.

The icing on the cake was that she took down the one picture she had in her corner office from her time spent working with none other than The Jordan brand and replaced it with the gift from me.

Only a well chosen gift can release that kind of power and response. Are you making calls to prospects and sending out brochures without getting the desired response? Tap into the currency of treasure and send out a gift that is worth talking about.

Not only will that person want to talk with you, but they will continue talking about it with the other leaders around them that you would love to be talking with as well. Compliments are appreciated and hand written notes are remembered, but well-chosen gifts are talked about with others and never forgotten.

Start thinking today, "Who is it that I currently have in my radar and to whom do I need to connect? Which of these contacts do I need to surprise with the currency of treasure? What is the treasure they would love to receive?"

With "The Three Currencies of Life," you can leverage the place upon which you stand. They are not something to be bragged about or to grow one's ego, but gifts to be used to bless others. I am excited for the doors these currencies will open in your life. With this power comes the opportunity to create more for yourself or to create awareness and open doors for others.

It is when the power of these currencies take hold that amazing things start to happen.

The challenge we all subconsciously face is that there is a finite amount of time and we don't want to waste time on something that is not truly benefiting ourselves or others. Investing these currencies, I was able to go from a business "no one" to a business number one.

The same will hold true for you.

---

## Summary Points

- Time is a currency, and its value depends on how we invest it.

- If you are spending time networking, be sure to stop and ask, "Who am I connecting with?"

- Model the wisdom of successful people to avoid mistakes.

- Many times the people we serve end up teaching us much more than we teach them.

- Our ability to love increases when we take time to love others.

- Giving a gift in business is not meant to create an action, but to solidify in the receiver's mind who you are, creating a strongly rooted positive memory.

- The best compliment you can give to a business person is a referral or connection.

- Well chosen gifts are talked about with others and never forgotten.

Jon Vroman began his professional career with Vector Marketing in 1994 as a sales representative for Cutco kitchen knives and quickly rose through the ranks to the position of North American Sales Promotion Manger. For over a decade now, Jon has spoken to over 50,000 business professionals and conducted over 2,000 coaching sessions throughout the US and Canada. Jon specializes in helping people attain high levels of personal and professional growth through his coaching and speaking. www.jonvroman.com Jon co-founded the charitable organization *Front Row Foundation* in 2005. In an effort to raise funds for his organization, Jon has completed three marathons, two of which were ultra marathons. Jon is happily married and lives in Virginia.

# Grow

## Jon Vroman

Some of our greatest lessons about growth and relationships can be taken from nature.

Emerson said, "All nature is the rapid efflux of goodness executing and organizing itself."

This sounds like the type of life and business I'd like to create. How about you? In this chapter, we'll cover two subjects. First, the power in connecting with others in order to develop a strong network. The other is personal growth - how your personal development positively affects your peer group and conversely how your peer group affects you.

I will illustrate how establishing a strong personal network and developing your own character and personality feed off each other and are essential to creating a successful life.

Two major events have shaped my passion for self-development and establishing my network.

First, I was born and raised in a military family, which meant I moved every two to three years and if I wanted friends, I needed to learn how to make them fast. I consciously developed the skills necessary to adapt to my environment at a very young age.

Luckily by age 15, I was pretty good at making friends. That was particularly helpful because that year I was told by doctors that I had the bone-age of a nine year old.

In junior high, I looked like I should have been in elementary school and was actually given growth hormones in order to stimulate cell reproduction and growth. In order to avoid being picked on, my desire to develop relationships (i.e. make friends) in some ways felt like a means of survival.

My plan was to befriend the biggest guy in school, which was exactly what I did, and this is when my earliest relationship skills were developed.

> *Life has a unique way of teaching us lessons.*
> *I believe that one method is, "Feather, Brick, Truck."*
> *It means that when life wants to teach you a lesson, it touches you lightly with a feather.*
> *If by chance you don't get the message the first time, life sends the message in the form of a brick.*
> *And if by chance you're so stubborn you still don't get the message, life has no choice but to hit you with a truck.*
> *It is wise to pay close attention to the feathers you encounter in life to avoid as many bricks and trucks as possible.*

Because I was vertically challenged, my first obsession with growth was that of a physical nature. I would beg my parents to measure my height on a regular basis behind the laundry room door and we would mark the wall if there was any progress.

Later in life, I came to realize that my happiness was not based on my physical growth, but rather on the growth of my character and personality. In any case, I felt as if "growing" kept coming up in my life at various stages and ages and was a recurring theme.

My insatiable appetite for personal growth came largely through the influence of my peer group and has, to date, been the biggest contributing factor to the personal and professional success I have enjoyed.

I started selling Cutco knives at age 19. Through my 14 year career with Vector, I never broke major sales records or held a Silver Cup in my hands; however , I was honored to receive the Dr. Steven Renner Memorial Award for Personal and Professional Growth.

For the record, this memorial award was created to recognize one manager within the team that demonstrated the most exceptional and positive growth for that specific year.

Dr. Steven Renner was a remarkable man who sold Cutco knives while paying his way through Medical school. He was an outstanding human being with a passion for life and helping others. His life was sadly taken in a car accident, but his legacy has continued to positively impact many people.

My personal and professional growth was largely due to the relationships I had developed with my mentors and colleagues at Vector.

Looking back, it's now easy to see that Vector not only helped me mature as a businessman, but this amazing company provided a home for me as well - a home stocked with supportive, loving friends.

Choosing the right environment is essential to one's success. Who are you being influenced by? Are your friends, co-workers, significant other or mentors helping you to be your best?

I personally believe that a true friend accepts you for not only who you are, but even more for whom you were born to be, your best self. We don't always act at our best, so having the right group to hold you accountable is essential.

## Building Powerful Relationships

*"Finding the right relationship is not so much about finding the right person as much as it is about becoming the right person."*
                                                                        *-- Jon Vroman*

In my own personal experience, having a strong network has been the most valuable aspect of my career and the most significant way in which I've found true happiness.

Ralph Waldo Emerson said, "The creation of a thousand forests is in one acorn."

I believe that one person has the power to multiply his efforts by creating a powerful network consisting of thousands of individuals.

What would happen if you were to take the ten most successful people and/or businesses in your immediate community and reach out to them?

In my late twenties, I made a conscious decision to make contact with a seemingly "untouchable person." I decided to write a birthday letter to my greatest mentor in the area of personal growth, Tony Robbins.

He got the letter, read it and a few weeks later I received a phone call from his organization letting me know that Tony wanted to include me in a book about people who had transformed their lives.

As I write this today, I don't know whether the book will ever be published or not, and to be honest, it doesn't really matter. What matters most is that I took the step to write a letter. And Tony read it!

My philosophy is this - no person, place or thing is out of my reach.

I challenge you to make contact with big clients, write to important people and reach out to the untouchable because you just might surprise yourself with whom you'll be able to connect.

Remember that you're just a few letters, phone calls or meetings away from your most significant future relationships. Who can you write a letter to today?

Creating great relationships begins with caring genuinely for people and wanting what's best for them. Here are six simple ways to show you care about people. They don't take a tremendous amount of time and you can start doing them today.

1. **Remember Birthdays** – I currently have hundreds of birthdays in my contact list and rarely does a day go by where I'm not calling someone to sing a painfully off key rendition of "Happy Birthday." Think about it - you're recognizing the moment they were brought into this world. Could there be a more significant day in their life?

2. **Send Handwritten Cards** – There's nothing like getting a handwritten card in the mail. They only take a few minutes to write, but can truly brighten someone's day. I keep every personal card sent to me. I literally have files and files of cards in my safe. They are truly my most treasured possessions. Every so often, I'll sit down and read through them. This fills me up in incredible ways. When you put something in writing, it has the ability to give and give and give. Try sending just one a day. I also recommend looking into www.thankyoucardmagic.com

3. **Remember names** – At one point in my life, I was horrible with names. Then I met Jim Stitt, CEO of ALCAS Corporation, which owns Cutco. We were traveling together with a large group on a business trip and at our departure gate in the airport he said, "Hey Jon, how are you?" I froze, and then actually said out loud, "You know my name?" Jim replied, "Of course I do, you're a very important person." That moment stuck with me for a very long time. If you'd like to improve your ability to remember names, I highly recommend the book *Remember Every Name Every Time* by Benjamin Levy. My skills have improved drastically in this area since reading it and have paid great dividends in establishing key relationships.

4. **Document Important People, Places and Things about Friends & Clients** – I learned early in my knife-selling career to

spend two to three minutes immediately after I left a customer's house to write down their dog's name, other products they liked or when their son or daughter was graduating school. When I called on them later, I would immediately have a rapport with them because I knew key information about their lives. You don't need to remember every detail about every person's life, but being able to remember the most important ones really shows you care. Knowing which things to remember will be easier if you pay close attention to the following suggestion...

5.  **Ask good questions and listen closely to the answers** – In a moment, I'm going to share with you my secret rapport building question; however, questions in general are essential to quality conversation. To this day, I often start coaching calls by asking, "So tell me what are the most exciting and challenging events in your life right now?" Rather than always trying to give advice, try asking questions and then just listen.

    My greatest work mentor, John Kane, taught me everything I know about good communication and he did so through his actions. During one specific conversation, John didn't say much, he just asked questions. At the end, I stood up and said, "That was the <u>best</u> conversation we've ever had." Interestingly, the conversation merely consisted of John asking questions while I did all the talking. John listened actively to each response and rather than giving great advice, which I knew he had, he just bit his tongue and asked another question.

    The lesson is this - people want to be heard. Next time you have the chance, look at whomever you are speaking to in the eye, whether it is your customer, your employee or your significant other and ask sincere questions. Then listen intently. You'll be amazed at how they light up. You may have heard it before, but we've been given two eyes, two ears and only one mouth because we're supposed to listen twice as much as we speak.

## The Secret Question

I find quite often that people ask questions for which they really don't care to know the answers. I have certainly been guilty of that myself.

A few years ago, I thought, "What question could I ask that would cut through the fluff and get to what matters most?"

That question is, "What's the question that you wish people would ask you, but they don't?" The first time I used this question, it was a huge success. I'll use an example of a conversation I had with an acquaintance named Tim.

Tim is a friend I speak with several times a year. Our conversations don't get too deep, often they're very topical. This time I wanted to try out my new question.

"So Tim, what's the question that you wish people would ask you, but they don't?"

Tim responded, "Wow, that's a really good question."

He paused and thought for a minute.

"Most people ask me about my kids and trust me Jon, I love my kids, but I'm really passionate about tennis. I really wish people would ask me about my tennis game more often."

"So Tim, tell me about your tennis game!" I said.

"That's clever," he chuckled. Then, he lit up as he talked about his favorite subject.

Trust me when I say this question by far has achieved more positive results than any question I have ever asked.


## 60 Second Brag Session

Here is another quality conversation-starter to be used with people you know.

When I take a call from a good friend but don't have time for a 15 minute conversation, I'll often say, "Hey Hal, I only have a few minutes but I'm really excited to hear about what's new with your life.

I would love a 60 second update, like a brag session, until we can catch up later."

Your friends can cover a lot in 60 seconds, trust me.

I also believe that it's nice when someone says, "Brag to me about all that's great in your life."

Remember that it's not always about how much time you spend with a person, but the quality of the time spent. Be authentic and sincere in your communications and watch your relationships blossom. If you don't have time to communicate all the details, you can at least communicate that you care.

> *If you don't have time to communicate all the details, you can at least communicate that you care.*

## Adapting To And Respecting Others

No matter what type of sunlight and water you provide for an acorn, it will never grow up to be a pine tree. My point is, we're all unique and different and we can't change who we are at our core.

When we learn who we are, we often make the mistake of separating ourselves from others who are not like us. By doing this, we get trapped in a very limited network and miss out on countless relationships. People often miss out on great relationships because they believe they must abandon who they are in order to associate with different people.

That's just not true.

In Japan, it's part of the culture to remove your shoes when entering someone's home. If I don't remove my shoes in my own house, but agree to when I'm in someone else's house, it is because it's their rule. I'm not being "untrue to my own beliefs." I'm merely being respectful of others. Our world is a beautiful place with many different types of people. Our network should be filled with a colorful variety of personalities with different values and beliefs.

In sales, we must often be flexible to build rapport, not because we're doing it only to make the sale, but because it's part of respecting others. It's part of being human. Think about how you can create a colorful portfolio of friends and contacts in your business and life.

## Personal Growth

*Education is not the filling of a pail, but the lighting of a fire.*
*-- -William Butler Yeats*


J. K. Rowling, famed author of the Harry Potter series, once said, "It matters not what someone is born, but what they grow to be."

Within each and every one of us are seeds of greatness.

Just like an acorn seed, the oak tree lives within, ready to be born into its place in the world. In order to flourish, the seed requires what most other living things need as well, the right environment to grow. Your relationships, your job, your hobbies and your health all need the right environment to grow.

When it comes to environment, I believe that one of the most important questions you can ask and answer is, "Who is in your peer group?" Who are you being influenced by and who are you influencing?

I love the saying, "If you hang out in a barber shop long enough, you're bound to get a hair cut." No matter how hard you try to resist changing, you will always be influenced to some degree by the people you associate with.

If I had to sum it up, I would offer this advice - Love your family unconditionally, but choose your friends carefully.

Being intentional about who you're being influenced by is a wise strategy. If you want to learn to golf, why not watch Tiger Woods? If you want to become a successful investor, I've got 62 billion reasons why you should emulate Warren Buffett. Learning to do what others do to become successful is called "modeling." In your life and business, choosing to model the right people is of utmost importance.

In fact, it could be the most important.

I've studied and researched the most successful salespeople in the world for over a decade now and one thing is for certain, they've all had successful role models. Essentially, we can all benefit by modeling others. You do not have to reinvent the wheel. Who are your top three role models? How can you learn from them on a deeper level?

At the end of every year, I list the 30 people I want to keep in my immediate sphere of influence. Being intentional about whom you spend time with is essential to success. Who would be in your top 30?

---

*Challenges help define who we are.*

*It's often times through adversity that we develop our strongest roots and our deepest character. There's no question that rejection comes with the territory in the sales field and can be difficult to deal with. Trees that are never exposed to wind develop shallow roots. It's when the wind blows that trees learn to anchor themselves tight, so when a severe storm comes through, they have the strength to survive.*

*Additionally, when it does rain, trees ultimately benefit from heavy rains. When it rains hard, the water gets deep into the earth and the roots of the tree stretch further into the soil. If it only rains lightly, then the roots stay closer to the surface for the water.*

*Similarly, if you find yourself in a period of life which feels like a storm is upon you, if you feel overwhelmed, drowning a bit or being pressed to your limits by the winds of change, just think of it as stretching your roots deeper into the ground so that you may be stronger in the end.*

---

## Growth Meets Relationships

To sum up - personal growth leads to great relationships and great relationships lead to further personal growth.

Here is a real-life example to illustrate my point. A few years ago I met Professor Ron Roberts from Penn State University. Professor Roberts also owns a training company, which Vector paid to conduct team-building programs for over 1,000 Cutco sales representatives and managers.

Because of the great relationship I created with Ron, I was asked to be a guest speaker in his Leadership and Motivation Class at Penn State. My relationship with Ron helped open doors in a career field in which I was intensely interested.

When I spoke at Penn State, Ron asked that I reference my own personal achievements, which at the time included reaching the position of North American Sales Promotion Manager within Vector by age 27, running several marathons, two of which were ultra marathons and starting a successful charitable organization, The Front Row Foundation.

Several students wanted to chat with me after the class. I was beginning to see how my personal growth was affecting others who wanted to become part of my network.

> *If a tree is not healthy, it cannot produce oxygen and bear fruit among many other contributions.*
> *The stronger the tree, the more it provides to others.*
> *The stronger we become as individuals, the more we provide more to others.*
> *The more we provide to others, our value to them rises.*
> *People want to be around people who add value to their lives.*

At the end of the speech, students were anxious to get my business card, join my foundation or learn about selling knives. It all began with my relationship with Ron, which led to my speaking at Penn State, which led to further relationships....and who knows where it will end!!

Once the ball starts rolling, it can gain momentum quickly. This all begs the question of which is more important - good relationships or personal growth? I believe a combination of the two is the right answer. Each feeds off the other.

We grow to give. When my life and business really took off I realized that the world was not about me, it was about "we." It's about becoming the best I can be so I can be the best for the group.

*Dr. Stanley Milgram, a noted social psychologist, was known for his work with the small-world experiment while at Harvard in 1967. Milgram's experiment developed out of a desire to learn more about the probability that two randomly selected people would somehow be connected to one another. In the experiment, Milgram sent envelopes to 160 random people living in various cities within the United States asking them to forward the package to a friend or acquaintance who they thought would be closer to a designated final individual.*

*The letter that was sent contained special instructions. Essentially, they said - If you don't know the individual who is the final target on a personal basis, do not try to contact them directly. Instead, send this package to a friend of yours who is more likely than you to know the target person."*

*Milgram discovered that the majority of the letters made it to the broker after passing through five or six different people. This experiment is the source of the more popularly known "six degrees of separation" concept. This rapidly spreading idea was at the center of a unique game called six degrees of Kevin Bacon. Interestingly enough, in January 2007, Kevin Bacon started a charitable organization around this concept which is fueled by the idea that we're all somehow closely connected. I believe whether it's 6, 10 or 20 degrees of separation, we're ultimately more closely connected than we believe.*

Said another way, while personal growth is important, how fulfilling a life would you lead if you were the best in your industry - "numero uno", silver cup champion, top of the class - but had few friends or family to celebrate with and took little time to enjoy your success?

The important thing is to be able to share whatever growth you experience with others. The growth and the network must go hand in hand.

## The Bonsai Tree And Mr. Miyagi

My favorite childhood movie was "The Karate Kid."

I know it's cheesy, but at age 10, I really liked it. This movie impacted my life in many ways. The basic story was about a teenage boy named Daniel, played by Ralph Macchio, who moves to a new city and gets picked on for being the new kid on the block.

After meeting his soon-to-be mentor, Mr. Miyagi, played by Noriyuki "Pat" Morita, he is taught how to find his own self esteem through the martial arts. Daniel's problem and Mr. Miyagi's willingness to teach were a perfect match.

One of my favorite scenes in the movie is when Mr. Miyagi invites Daniel into his workshop where he is pruning the bonsai trees. Mr. Miyagi asks Daniel if he'd like to try pruning one, but Daniel hesitates. Miyagi insists and gives Daniel a pair of pruning shears and the following conversation ensues.

"Danielson, close eye, trust, concentrate, think only tree," Miyagi tells him.

"Make a perfect picture down to last pine needle. Wipe mind clean of everything but tree. Nothing exist in whole world, only tree…You got it?"

Daniel shakes his head yes.

"Open eyes. Remember picture?"

"Yeah." Daniel says.

"Make like picture. Just trust picture"

"How do I know if my picture is the right one?" Daniel asks.

"If come from inside you, always right one."

What picture do you hold in your mind with respect to your personal growth and your relationships? Who were you born to be? What were you born to do? What types of people are destined to be your closest friends? Is it clear down to the tiniest detail? Trust that the picture that comes from within you is the right one.

Implement the strategies shared within this chapter and watch yourself and your network grow. Take time to think about who you want to be most like and spend time with them, either in person or perhaps by reading their books. Remember that nothing will influence your life more than the people you associate with and the books you read.

The happiest people on earth have found the balance between focusing on themselves and focusing on others. The wisdom comes from knowing which one needs your attention at any given time. Sometimes you'll need to put others on hold and focus on taking care of yourself. Other times, you must put your own needs aside and give everything you've got to others. Most days, we need to be "off-self" and "on-others."

Create your life, your relationships and your passions into something noble, and in the end, whatever it becomes will be perfect.

---

## Summary Points

- Who are you being influenced by? Pay attention to who is around you. We want those who hold us accountable to being our best.

- Finding the right relationship is not so much about finding the right person as much as it is about becoming the right person.

- You are just a few letters, phone calls or meetings away from your most significant future relationships.

- Remember to do the following: remember birthdays and names; send thank you cards; document important information about people; and ask great questions.

- Build rapport to show respect to others, not just to make a sale.

- Challenges define who we are.

- It is important to be able to share your personal growth that you experience with others.

- Hold a precise picture in your mind that defines what you want for your personal growth and your relationships.

Cecelia "Fi" Mazanke is a master certified leadership coach and founder of Direct Connect Coaching in St. Charles, Illinois. Fi started her coaching career in January, 2000. She has successfully worked with hundreds of clients in all walks of life helping them live a more fulfilled, purposeful and balanced lifestyle. Through her vision, the Leadership Coaching Program was established at Vector Marketing Corporation. Fi is certified in the Birkman Master's Program. She has been happily married for 19 years and has two beautiful children. Through coaching, Fi is living a passionate life and guiding others to live their dreams.

# It's My Life

## Fi Mazanke

*It's my life, it's now or never. I ain't gonna live forever. I just wanna live while I'm alive.*

- Bon Jovi

L ife is all about the choices we make.

Little did I know that in June of 1984, the choice I made to accept a job selling knives would forever forge a path in my life that would be so profound. I was 19.

I entered my job interview with an open heart and open mind, despite the very sparse office setting with green carpeting that buckled in its center. The interview was with a sharp-looking young District Manager who demonstrated the product professionally. I knew I wanted that set of knives, once I saw the Cutco knife zip through a piece of rope like it was melted butter and the shears cut through a penny.

I took the job as a Cutco Sales Representative.

With my sample kit under my arm, I set out to see how these knives would sell. I was quickly invited to attend a sales conference in the Chicago area. After much contemplation, I decided to go. It was there that I got my first valuable lesson in sales. I watched as ordinary people like me were recognized on stage for their outstanding sales achievements. My eyes opened wide to the possibilities that I had as a sales rep. I made a choice during that conference to apply the lessons I learned about selling and see what impact it would make on my results.

It worked - I set an office record in my first 10 days of sales.

My results continued and I had the opportunity to meet the Vice President of the company, Marty Domitrovich. Marty was a tall, strong build of a man, with a quiet, yet distinct voice. He had a presence about him - a caring attitude and deep knowledge of the business that other people looked to emulate. Marty was revered as the most beloved Cutco sales manager in the history of the company.

The company was looking to expand through young leaders, so I quickly moved into sales management. I worked a couple of summers as a sales manager, but realized that I didn't want to continue in the sales management end of the business. I made the choice to leave.

Something compelled me to call Marty and ask if I could meet to discuss my decision. I asked Marty for an exit interview and Marty, being a kind soul, granted my request. I was surprised at my request, because it was out of character for me. I wasn't accustomed to asking for what I wanted.

It turned out that listening to that inner nudge would be perfect for both Marty and me. During the exit lunch, I made a choice to share with Marty my desire for the job of Sales Promotion Manager. This position is responsible for arranging all meetings and conferences, writing newsletters and designing contests for the entire Central Region of the company.

Marty explained that the Sales Promotion Manager (SPM) position had been recently filled by a man who had more experience than me and that the company just moved him and his wife to Chicago from

Michigan. Marty seemed confident that the SPM job was set with the right man in place. I was disappointed that my ideal job was already filled and I realized that it was time for me to move on.

Shortly thereafter, I made a choice to take a part-time job in the Better Sportswear Department and Marshall Fields Department Store. This job choice granted me two things I needed: (1) the flexibility to look for full-time work and (2) the opportunity to build my career wardrobe at a discount.

My mom, who is a former cloister nun – that is, a nun who remains in seclusion in the convent - urged me to pray a novena to St. Teresa. A novena, a prayer said over nine consecutive days, is a pretty commonplace thing for former cloister nuns. I learned from her that having faith to solve all of life's problems, including finding a new job, was essential.

I decided to begin saying the novena to find the perfect job on my way to my new job, since the drive took 30 minutes, I felt a sense of peace when I said the novena. It was as if I was releasing the work of finding a job to a much greater power than me.

On the 7th day of saying my novena, I received a call from a familiar voice.

It was Marty. He asked me if I was still interested in the Sales Promotion Manager's position. "Yes, I was," I said. I was both elated and confused.

"What happened to Craig?"

"Craig was offered an opportunity to run a family ice cream parlor back in Michigan," Marty explained, "and he welcomed the chance to go home."

He and I scheduled an interview and he hired me on the spot!

I continued to say the novena as a form of gratitude for the miracle I'd received. I gently tucked away my experience with the novena, knowing that faith lead me to, at age 22, landing my ideal job.

Over the years, Marty taught me many valuable lessons.

## Bartering

To Marty, building lasting business relationships was essential to success. Marty incorporated bartering for Cutco into all of his business relationships. By having a product with superior quality like Cutco, people saw the benefits of owning the product.

I began to ask the "Marty prompted" question to all of my business contacts, "Do you barter?"

Eventually, the art of bartering became second nature to me. In fact, to this day, I barter my coaching services for goods and services such as sports memorabilia, massage, and even jewelry. Bartering is a valuable business tool.

## Negotiating

Another beneficial lesson I learned from Marty was the art of negotiating.

According to Marty, the key in negotiating is to ask for what you want and then shut up.

At first, this concept was uncomfortable to me. I was not used to asking for what I wanted. But Marty would nudge me along to keep asking for a long list of requests. I got accustomed to asking for free hotel rooms, hotel suite upgrades and complimentary food and beverage breaks.

One day, I even asked for the hotel to throw in a free continental breakfast for our 1,500 guests. You can imagine my surprise when the hotel sales manager said "yes" to that request.

I remember taking a company trip to Ixtapa, Mexico. Everything purchased in Mexico is negotiated and I had the experience of negotiating for Mexican handmade blankets. Of course, I consulted with Marty on which vendor was giving the best deals on blankets because he just negotiated a purchase. Well, I went to that same vendor and got my blankets for $2.00 less than Marty did.

I felt as if I graduated from Marty's "School of Negotiation."

Today, one of the first exercises I have my clients do, is to clearly ask for what they want. I remind them to take off all limitations from their asking because there are no limits except what exists in their minds.

I tell my clients they can realize the true potential of what they want to create once they can overcome the hurdle of removing any limits from their mind. Most people get stuck in the everyday details of life that they forget the asking step. We need to be reminded to "ask and you shall receive."

## Listening to Others

Listening goes hand-in-hand with asking.

Being an active listener was an important aspect of my Cutco training. I learned how to listen to the objections of customers and how to answer those objections. Listening is becoming a dying art form because of all of the distractions that exist in the world.

Just check out the advertisements you get when standing in line at the grocery store or pumping gas. The opportunities for silence become reduced as technology advances. Listening requires discipline and practice.

Effective listening happens when you are fully present, with no judgments or attachments to the outcome. My coaching practice, whether in person or on the phone, has enabled me to hone my listening skills over the years.

## Listening to Yourself

I believe, however, that to develop an expert level of listening, you must first begin listening to yourself.

What messages do you tell yourself on a daily basis? What thoughts are consistent in your mind about yourself, your co-workers and about your loved ones?

You can get valuable clues about how to propel your life in a more positive direction by paying attention to the mental chatter that occurs in your head on a daily basis. See what happens when you turn off the radio, television, phones or Blackberry. It's an interesting exercise to do laundry or dishes and be present with your thoughts. Notice what you feel like if you go to the gym or do your workout without an iPod.

Your inner world opens up to you to assist you in making new choices for yourself, once you unplug from the numerous distractions that the outside world offers. When I was working as a Sales Promotion Manager, I liked to go for walks in the morning. The walks were filled with a cluttered mindset of all of the things I had to accomplish that day. I would get out of bed and be attached to my "To Do" list without any real quality time in just being available to myself and what I wanted for my life. It was an automatic 0-60 as soon as my feet hit the floor about work and getting tasks done.

I hired a coach to create balance in my life. I noticed how unbalanced I had become. I forgot to listen to the inner messages I was receiving. One such message was that I needed time for myself. Another message was that I needed time with my husband. I found that my own needs were at the bottom of the list because I was distracted and focusing my time and energy on work and on my young children.

I also held a strong belief that I needed to work through the pain and exhaustion I was feeling at the time. I had a "just suck it up and do it" attitude. I was resisting the reality of what I felt in the moment. My pain increased to near deafening levels because I was resisting the truth.

My world all around me showed signs of this lack of balance and listening to my inner guidance system. My children were suffering from illnesses regularly. I was so sick at times that I lost my voice consistently and I became so weak that I didn't have enough strength to hold my children.

My coach introduced me to the concept of taking five minutes for myself everyday just to listen to my thoughts. I was shocked to reveal the suffering I was holding in my thoughts. I had read a statistic somewhere that we have 90,000 thoughts a day and 2/3 of those thoughts are negative. Boy was this true for me - I uncovered the main source of my negativity right in my head!

There were stories about the past and fears about the future, but never a focus of what wonders existed in the present moment. My new habit of taking a break and listening to my inner world was a positive habit and the results were tangible and real.

I found that as I was able to listen to my thoughts. I was also able to remain more present in listening to others more attentively. In sales and management, listening is one of the most important skills to develop.

Another internal message became evident as I progressed with my coach.

It was time for me to move into a new direction and leave my job as Sales Promotion Manager. With my husband just getting started in his own business, this move sounded like an impossible feat. The internal messages to leave my SPM job got louder over time and during one meeting in July of 1999, I knew I needed to make the leap.

I didn't have any direction to go, so I remembered my walk of faith as I got my job as Sales Promotion Manager. I remembered the novena, the faith from my mother. I trusted this was the right decision for me without having another job lined up. I was clear about a couple of things - I wanted a career where I helped people and I wanted to have a flexible work schedule with the ability to work from home and care for my young children.

On August 11, 1999, I told Marty it was time for me to leave my post as SPM.

I cried and fretted about the future. Amazingly enough, about 2 weeks after I told Marty of my decision to leave, my coach shared with me a program to become certified as a coach. It felt perfect and I accepted the opportunity with Marty's blessing. He even encouraged me to bring coaching in to the Central Region on an experimental basis for the first year.

I found a new path and I began my coaching career in January of 2000.

The program was so successful in our region, that after the first year, I was in negotiations to become the National Leadership Coach.

Selling Cutco certainly enabled me to find yet another perfect position in my life.

## Listening to & Re-Framing Internal Messages

In coaching clients over the past 9 years, I've realized that people look to escape the pain and judgments of their own thoughts by trying to numb those thoughts through distractions. People use many different methods to drown out hearing their own thoughts.

Here's what I know - you become the observer of your own thoughts, once you begin to be aware and listen to your inner messages. Here's how to do it:

First, detach from the story of your thoughts and just watch them unfold, just as if you are watching a movie. Then, when you don't like the messages you are getting, shift them by saying, "Cancel. Release." You then replace the thought with what you would like to create.

If you are looking for a parking space and you start to get negative about finding a space, listen to your thoughts. Are your thoughts getting you closer to creating a parking space or further away? If you are getting closer, continue and voice out loud your desire to get a perfect parking space. If you are getting further away from creating a parking space, cancel and release the thoughts and replace them with what you really want.

I love seeing the success that happens when clients learn to be aware of their thoughts and then change their minds. After we see success with parking spaces, we up the ante a bit and create success in other areas beyond parking lots

I once had a client with whom I worked a few times. He was accustomed to listening to the inner messages that were driving his life. He said that his business was struggling and so he paid attention to what he was saying to himself.

"Why is the business not improving?" He asked himself everyday.

He was very excited to call me one day and tell me he had been asking himself the wrong question all along. His focus was on what was going wrong with the business. He was holding himself and his business trapped in the role of the victim.

After listening to his own thoughts, he shifted the question.

Now, he asked himself, "How can I impact the business?" and "What can I do to generate more business?"

Just by shifting his questions from victimization to empowerment, he was able to generate new ideas to increase his business. It paid off for this client to be aware of his thoughts. Listening to those subtle, yet powerful inner messages can impact your sales on a daily basis, but it requires asking a question and listening for the answer.

Once you start the practice of listening to and then observing your thoughts, you can recognize that you aren't your thoughts, but rather the one who is observing your thoughts. Afterwards, you can release thoughts and allow space for inspiring ideas to occur. Inspiring thoughts are those grand ideas that just seem to appear out of thin air.

It's those times where you shout, "I've got the best idea!"

You've allowed your spirit to come forth. You are in spirit when you are inspired.

## Setting Intentions

After asking for what you want and listening to your inner messages, one of my favorite skills to practice is setting intentions. I consider myself a "setting intentions" junkie.

I first learned about setting intentions after listening to a tape series by Jerry and Ester Hicks, a self-help couple who have authored numerous books. Intention setting is different than goal setting because goal setting is more about an outer target.

To intend, in this sense, means "to tend to" what is inside of you. That's why inner listening is so important. You can have a clear understanding of your intentions when you listen to what you want. Then, you can take action on the inner desire and fulfill your intention. Intentions allow us to create what is desired within us.

I started to have success in setting intentions in my life. I saw so many positive results that I began teaching the art of setting intentions to my clients. Over the years, I have witnessed clients successfully set intentions for perfect office space, for more new business, for specific types of customers or patients for ideal jobs and even for their ideal mate. Clients begin to listen to those inner messages so that they can feel empowered to set clear intentions in their lives.

In my own life, I had a seemingly unsuccessful attempt at setting intentions. In November of 2007, tickets went on sale for the Bon Jovi concert in Chicago. Chris Daughtry was the opening act and my son loves Chris Daughtry. I thought it would be a fun Christmas present for him.

I set my intentions to get tickets. I searched on-line right as tickets went on sale. I was disappointed to find my intentions were not fulfilled. I felt extreme disappointment. I knew that intentions don't always work the way we expect.

I released the attachment to the outcome by simply saying, "If it's for the highest good that Jake and I to go to the concert, it'll happen." That's it. If it's for the highest good, it'll be allowed to happen.

I didn't know how it would happen, but I just trusted the process. I let it go.

One day, about a month later, I mentioned my lack of success about the tickets to a friend of mine. She has some connections in the music business, and she wished I had asked her for the tickets. I didn't want to impose on her. My failure to not have my intentions fulfilled was the best thing that could have happened to me because for my birthday, I got a card. The card said that on February 24, 2008, I was to go to the will call at the United Center in Chicago and pick up not two, but four tickets to the concert.

Not only was I able to enjoy the concert with Jake, but I brought my husband and daughter along.

We celebrated my December birthday at the Bon Jovi concert in February as a family. It was one of the most memorable nights we ever had as a family, as we were all together enjoying the music of Daughtry and Bon Jovi.

I truly believe that because I released the attachment to the outcome, I got the greatest benefits of my intention. Setting intentions in sales can be as easy as being provided with the best customers, making a connection on the phone, or even making a sale.

It's a great practice to set intentions daily.

I am now living the life of my dreams. I have a thriving career as a Leadership Coach and guiding others to live the life of their dreams. My life feels balanced and genuine as I take time for myself, my family, my relationships, work and most importantly, fun. This fulfillment that I feel would have never happened if I didn't answer an ad back in June of 1984 to begin selling knives.

For that, I am eternally grateful.

Ask yourself:
1. What choices are you currently making? Are those choices getting you closer to or further away from where you want to be?
2. What happens when you put your awareness on your thoughts?
3. Can you begin to focus your thoughts on what you want?
4. What do you desire to create?
5. How can you set your intentions daily?

---

## Summary Points

- Life is all about the choices we make.

- The power of faithful prayer is limitless.

- It is important to ask for what we want, and to remove self imposed limits on our asking.

- Effective listening happens when you are fully present, with no judgments or attachments to the outcome.

- Taking time to listen to our own internal thoughts leads to tangible and real results.

- Listening to our thoughts develops the skill of taking action on and fulfilling our inner intentions and desires.

- When we release our attachment to an outcome, we create the opportunity for an even greater outcome.

Ranjeet Pawar graduated in 1998 from the nation's number one Entrepreneurship Program, Babson College, with a double major in Entrepreneurship and Marketing. He is Founder and Director of Monsoon Gallery, one of the Northeast's most well-respected fine art galleries. Ranjeet sat on various committees, boards and commissions, including those for the Southside Film Festival, Downtown Business Association and Bethlehem Fine Arts Commission. When not working on his next entrepreneurial venture, Ranjeet spends his time traveling the world and capturing its nuances through the power of the lens. For more information, visit his website at www.RanjeetPawar.com.

# Impassioned Convictions
# Guide Successful Entrepreneurs

Ranjeet Pawar

*"Be the change you wish to see in the world"*

Mohandas Gandhi

You may be asking yourself, what does Gandhi have to do with entrepreneurship? Well, I'd venture to say everything.

In 1979, India - the world's largest democracy - embarked in a new direction. My great grandfather, Choudhary Charan Singh, was elected to the post of Prime Minister. At the time, I was too young to truly appreciate the weight of his title. But I did know that my great grandfather was considered a leader of his people and that he had been considered a leader all his life.

As I grew older, and consequently more aware of the world around me, I realized the stories of his life profoundly affected me. To be more precise, they inspired me to change my entire outlook on the way I saw my life and its place in the world.

My life had the ability to affect positive change. And since the success of that rested solely upon me, I could not afford to be anything other than a leader.

That being said, it's important to note that leadership is not a learned trait. It comes from something much more visceral. Leadership comes from one's passion for excellence. It comes from the deep understanding that leading people is more about responsibility than it is about accomplishment.

Because of our narrowed understanding of what it means to be successful, we've become accustomed to associating successful entrepreneurship with the high value of an Initial Public Offering. It's as though we've forgotten that new ventures are rarely born from anything more than the intense desire to provide a good or service to those that cannot live without it.

True success is found when one awakens their entrepreneurial spirit and creates something of value.

I first learned of the true power of the entrepreneurial spirit while attending Babson College in Wellesley, Massachusetts. Professor Stephen Spinelli stood before us on our first day and said something that utterly confused me.

"If you are here to learn entrepreneurship so that you can become wealthy," he began, "then you are in the wrong field. Entrepreneurs don't create wealth, they simply create."

The class was Introduction to Entrepreneurship and the notion fascinated me during my time at Babson. I went about my years and learned a great deal about industry analysis, corporate multi-business strategies, core competency assessments and so on and so forth. But it wasn't until I drew the parallel between entrepreneurship and leadership that it all made sense.

Entrepreneurship isn't solely driven by the goal of creating wealth. If that were the case, then much of what we take for granted in the world might never have even taken shape.

Douglas Engelbart, for example, designed the first computer mouse in 1964. And yet it had not found its way into people's homes until 1981. In entrepreneurship, it's necessity - not money - that breeds the creative mindset.

> *True success is found when one awakens their entrepreneurial spirit and creates something of value.*

The prospect of wealth isn't fully abundant until well after an entrepreneurial venture has already been set in motion. Many of the world's most accomplished entrepreneurs are more driven by the passion to institute change than they are by the desire to create wealth.

A wonderful example of this can be found in the life's work of Muhammad Yunus.

In 1974, he entered into the banking industry by loaning 42 Bangladeshi women $27 to buy raw materials needed to bring items to market. The endeavor proved fruitful for all parties involved. Yunus received his money back, plus interest, while each of the 42 women had overcome the financial barriers impeding them from entering the marketplace.

His success eventually led to the inception of the Grameen Bank in 1983. The bank was founded on the principle of aiding the poor of Bangladesh in an effort to enrich their lives and the community in which they live. The bank has loaned more than $7 billion in funds to more than seven million people (97% of whom are women).

In Bangladesh, the bank has played an integral role in lifting the poor out of a seemingly unbreakable cycle of despair and placing them on the path to building a stronger and more viable future.

You may consider Yunus's microfinance model to be nothing more than a warm-hearted story of triumph over adversity. But before you pass him over as nothing more than a well-intentioned philanthropist, consider this - Muhammad Yunus's $27 venture positioned him to be the foremost authority on microfinance's effects on poverty.

Since 1974, he has written numerous bestsellers, been covered in countless media outlets, and won over 80 prestigious awards in more than 20 different countries, including the 2006 Nobel Peace Price.

He's done fairly well for $27.

When Gandhi wrote, "Be the change you wish to see in the world," he inadvertently laid down a foundation for all impassioned entrepreneurs to build upon:

1.  Always have strong convictions supporting your ideas
2.  Maintain relentless work ethics when trying to achieve your goals
3.  Never settle for anything other than the best

My life is driven by the sense that I have a responsibility to create positive change in the world.

And it's a belief system that I draw upon when I move from one challenge to the next.

## Successful Entrepreneurs Establish Awe-Inspiring Goals

*"Dream big and dare to fail."*

-- Norman Vaughan

In 1994, an 89-year-old adventurer named Norman Vaughan set out to climb to the top of a 10,302-foot tall mountain in Antarctica.

He was asked why he attempted to accomplish such a tremendous feat at his age.

"I always dream big and dare myself to fail," he answered with conviction.

His philosophy was simple - set your goals higher than what you think is achievable, and then achieve it.

Accomplished entrepreneurs are successful because they do not accept that their limits, whatever they may be, are insurmountable. Successful entrepreneurs force themselves to improve their skill sets and conquer their weaknesses by daring themselves to accomplish a project they are more likely to fail than realize. This is why they never fall victim to complacency.

In 1988 my father started his company, Summit Manufacturing, with the goal of becoming one of the strongest high-mast steel pole producers in the industry, a truly daring prospect when considering that at the end of his first year in business, the company had produced a total of one pole.

He couldn't risk getting laid off again and this motivated him.

He had a family to worry about and at the age of 44 he couldn't afford to take a chance on someone else's leadership again. My father invested most of the family's money into Summit Manufacturing because he was driven by the need for a better life and more secure future.

Becoming an industry leader was non-negotiable.

Rajendra Pawar wasn't merely going to succeed in his industry, he was going conquer his industry.

So over the next nine years, he put his tenacity behind his goal and grew the company to the 4th largest high-mast steel pole manufacturer in the industry. By 1998, his resolve had turned into much more than he ever expected when Berwind Financial, LP offered him and his investors more than $40 million for the company.

My father sold Summit Manufacturing. Later that year, he was honored by Ernst & Young as *Entrepreneur of the Year* in the manufacturing sector of Pennsylvania.

Of course there are numerous factors that propelled him to that level of success, but none of these factors alone were the defining cause. It's important to understand that garnering a marketing degree and developing an acute sense of creative sales tactics are not at the heart of an entrepreneur's success. Those are all qualifications that can always be learned over time. And where would the differentiation be if we all held the same credentials?

> *Accomplished entrepreneurs are successful because*
> *they do not accept that their limits,*
> *whatever they may be, are insurmountable.*
> *Successful entrepreneurs force themselves to improve*
> *their skill sets and conquer their weaknesses by*
> *daring themselves to accomplish a project they are*
> *more likely to fail than realize.*

The distinguishing characteristic that sets one entrepreneur apart from another is in the intensity of their approach. I would consider any other measure of a successful entrepreneur to be "conceptually flawed."

My father was passionate about his company. He demanded from himself an unwavering focus on the end goal. And while he kept a keen eye on the bottom line, he was never distracted by the perceived value that his company may have had on the open market.

He followed Spinelli's first lesson from Introduction to Entrepreneurship - he didn't create Summit Manufacturing to create significant wealth. The wealth came because of his impassioned spirit and intense conviction to succeed.

> *The distinguishing characteristic that sets one entrepreneur*
> *apart from another is in the intensity of their approach.*
> *I would consider any other measure of a successful*
> *entrepreneur to be "conceptually flawed."*

A little bit about the company that bought my Dad's business -Berwind Financial was a multi-faceted organization dealing in various industries with billions of dollars at its disposal. Its core business was identifying and investing within profitable companies. It was assumed they were strategically poised to turn their purchase into a highly profitable investment.

However, by 2002, Summit Manufacturing was forced to declare bankruptcy.

Fortunately for my father, this worked to his advantage. He was such an awful retiree, that when this opportunity lay before him, his entrepreneurial spirit couldn't pass it up. He went to the negotiating table, gave them his best offer and reacquired Summit Manufacturing for approximately $4 million.

Rajendra Pawar entered the market - with his newly renamed company, PennSummit Tubular - with even more conviction than before.

He was driven by the desire to reposition his old company to its rightful place at the top of the industry. But the company was plagued with low market value and poor standing amongst suppliers and customers. My father would have to rebuild from the ground up.

My father put his tenacity behind his goal and grew PennSummit Tubular to the 3rd largest high-mast steel pole manufacturer in the industry. By the end of 2007, his resolve paid off again, when Valmont Industries, the industry's largest pole manufacturer, offered him substantially more for the company than Berwind had in 1998. He sold the company again, knowing that Valmont Industries would never allow his dream to fall away as Berwind Financial had.

In 2008, Raj Pawar was recognized by the Northeast Pennsylvania Manufacturers' and Employers' Association and received an award for *Manufacturing Excellence*. He was recognized by the prestigious Ben Franklin Technology Partners of Northeastern Pennsylvania and received the Ben Franklin iExchange 2008 *Innovation Award for Manufacturing and Achievement*.

Rajendra Pawar emigrated from India in the late 1960's with only $8 dollars in his pocket and the promise of one day achieving the American Dream. My father dared himself to fail by dreaming he could achieve the American Dream.

Well, he did. Twice.

When Vaughan climbed that 10,302-foot tall mountain in Antarctica, he expressed the most essential tenet needed for an entrepreneur to reach his fullest potential - set your goals higher than what you think is achievable, and stop at nothing to achieve them.

I want only the best for myself. When I set my goals high, I insure that I will not allow myself to settle for anything less.

## Creative Ventures Generate Creative Opportunities

*My life is my art.*
-- Ranjeet Pawar

I spent my summers working at my father's manufacturing facility. He insisted I learn the value of developing a strong work ethic. And what better way than to do that than to wear a pair of steel-toed boots and breathe in the fumes of freshly-welded steel!

My time at the plant did teach me a great deal about the importance of maintaining a strong work ethic. The true value of the experience, however, was more intricate than that.

I learned that my goals, no matter what they were, could only be reached through the incorporation of teamwork.

At no time was this more obvious than when I was 19. I decided to expand on my professional skills and took an opportunity to work for Vector Marketing as a Cutco Sales Representative. The concept of Vector was alluring.

I was to take the reins of my own company by operating as an independent contractor and take the world by storm.

I nurtured strong leadership skills at Vector and set numerous sales records locally and regionally. I reaffirmed my intense desire to always be the best. But I could not have achieved a single one of my records without the help of my mentors and peers.

I needed a strong work ethic and the understanding that, as a leader, I needed to set my goals high. But if I had expected to bring all those pieces together, I needed to embrace the guidance and support of those around me.

> *...merely wishing the world would change isn't the same as actually creating the change.*

At Vector, I was provided with just such an experience.

Division managers and corporate executives took notice of my accomplishments and offered me my own branch with the opportunity to grow vertically within the organization. However, my time with Vector was not a long one. I left just six months after I started. I was bringing home larger paychecks than my father and he owned his own multi-million dollar company.

But money wasn't what drove me to be a part of Vector. I was driven by the opportunity to be one of the best in the organization. And as I pointed out earlier, success comes from the passionate desire to push yourself beyond your perceived limits.

I became one of the top sales representatives in an international corporation that employs thousands. Vector Marketing was a highly valuable experience that increased my viability as a business professional. Their business model challenged me because it forced me to work with others while having to answer to myself. On a given day, I had to deal with various types of people and because each was different in their-own way, I had to develop a creative way to identify with my market base.

I became masterful at communicating and acquired a talent for customer relations and service.

I eventually found my calling in the art industry and opened a fine art gallery in Bethlehem, Pennsylvania called "Monsoon." My business grew from the idea that if people did not have the ability to travel the world to experience its differing cultures, then perhaps artistic expressions of those cultures should be brought to them.

Financially speaking, a fine art gallery is far from being a cash cow. It's unique in that it's a product-driven company that's completely service-dependent. The success of Monsoon Gallery depends entirely upon the strength of its name. As a result, I honed my marketing skills and quickly became a public relations aficionado.

Since 2003, the gallery has been covered nearly 100 times in local, national and international media outlets. The exposure resulted in the respect of both potential clients and potential business partners. I have been asked to sit on various committees, boards and commissions, and since Monsoon's opening, I have become intricately involved with city matters and developed a strong rapport with local mayors, senators and congressmen.

None of Monsoon's accomplishments would be visible today if not for the coordinated efforts of all those it touches. Monsoon's employees, artisans, clients and supporters, have all worked hand-in-hand to provide me with guidance and direction that have helped me achieve the goals I've set. My responsibility has been to recognize the teamwork that has been put forth and to harness the power of that teamwork so as to become a stronger and more effective leader.

I believe that leadership comes from the deep understanding that leading people is more about responsibility than it is about accomplishment. In giving back to my community, my entrepreneurial spirit takes a direct role in changing the world around me. If my life is my art, then how I live it depends upon what I put into it. And merely wishing the world would change isn't the same as actually creating the change.

I built Monsoon Gallery to position myself as a leader in my field. I surpassed that role and expanded my clout in a new industry. I have many more dreams I'd like to dare myself to achieve. My passions and convictions have prepared me to achieve these goals by being a leader in anything life brings my way.

My only question is: "Do you know what drives you?"

I dare you to do two things: (1) recognize the value of teamwork and (2) expect from your day to day what you expect from your life.

Accomplishments are not simply met the day that they are achieved. What I do every day is as important as the next time I reach a set goal.

And this is why my life is my art.

---

**Summary Points**

- Leadership is more about responsibility than it is about accomplishment.

- True success is found when someone awakens their entrepreneurial spirit and creates something of value.

- Accomplished entrepreneurs are successful because they do not accept that their limits, whatever they may be, are insurmountable.

- Wishing the world would change isn't the same as creating the change.

- The distinguishing characteristic that sets one entrepreneur apart from another is in the intensity of their approach.

- Set your goals higher than what you think is achievable, and stop at nothing to achieve them.

- Become an effective leader by harnessing the power of teamwork.

- Know what it is that drives you.

Jerry Liu graduated in 2000 with double-major degrees in Business Economics and Chinese Language and Literature from the University of Santa Barbara. Jerry also holds an MBA with an emphasis in Leadership. Jerry worked with over 2000 sales representatives as a District Manager for Cutco. In 2006, Jerry won the Silver Cup National Championship Trophy in 2006 with more than 100% growth over the prior year. Jerry is currently the CEO of the LIU Institute of Child Development and Co-chairman of the LIU Foundation for Autistic Children.

# Tao

## Jerry Liu

Lao Tzu, one of the earliest Chinese philosophers of health and longevity, wrote *The Book of Tao* 2,500 years ago. The literal translation of the *Tao* means "The Way." Chinese people believe there is much to be learned about health from the ways of the universe and the manner in which nature operates.

You can only be one with the "Tao" through observing the way of the universe and the practicing nature in your body. The Chinese refer to "the practicing of nature" as the movement of *Chi*, or natural energy, that flows through one's body. It is when the Tao is embodied in you that you are able to live your life to the maximum health.

I believe professional selling is "the Tao" to leadership and entrepreneurship success.

Much of leadership and entrepreneurship is learned through the true embodiment of sales attitude and skills. Once you have fully grasped the Tao of selling, the sales skills and attitude provide a framework for you to work with in leadership situations. It is only when you practice the

Tao in leadership situations that health and longevity will be ensured in your business and organization.

I came to America at the age of 11, not knowing a word of English. I lived with my aunt in a town that is predominately Chinese. Many people saw many reasons for me not to succeed. But I felt that my heritage offered me a unique outlook in the world of business and as a result, gave me a unique approach to management.

My name is Jerry Liu. It is a very difficult task for me to write about myself. I was taught at a young age that being humble is a virtue. This was ingrained in me by my Chinese parents. It is much easier for me to go straight into sales and leadership, but I believe that it is necessary for you to know a little about my background in order to lend credibility to the rest of the chapter.

I double-majored in Business Economics and Chinese Literature for my undergraduate studies. During my four years of college, I encountered a unique opportunity to sell knives starting the summer prior to my junior year.

Unknowingly at the time, this sales job gave me a set of tools that I later used again to recruit and organize a team that won the Silver Cup National Championship with the company. My MBA with an emphasis in leadership contributed tremendously to my academic knowledge of leadership and my experiences in sales and leadership provided concrete examples to support the academic concepts/theories.

This knife-selling job gave me the foundation to run my own business in the field of child development. I am currently operating over twenty learning centers in the US, Taiwan and China. My experience has led me to believe that skills and attitudes of sales are crucial to leadership success. I owe much of my success to the *Tao of Selling* .

In this chapter, I will identify six qualities of successful leaders.

If you are currently in sales, you need to take every opportunity to develop these character traits and skills. It will be absolutely worthwhile to develop these elements because we are embedded in a society where the power of influence is highly desirable.

If you are already in a leadership position, I will show you a different perspective on thinking about leadership and how to produce long-term results with the following characteristics.

**"Men is Earth, Earth is Universe, Universe is Tao, Tao is Nature" - Book of Tao**

## Traits One, Two and Three

By definition, an *organization* is two or more people with a common purpose.

Whether you are in a position of management, running a business or the head of bible study, you are leading an organization. These six traits that I will identify, I have personally learned through sales. The more experiences you have in developing these characteristics when in sales, the more apparent they will be when you are in a leadership position. In essence, these leadership principles are what I consider the ultimate sales principles.

## Integrity

Integrity is first and foremost.

As a Cutco sales rep in college, it would have been easy to tell my customers on the phone that I am doing a sales presentation for a "school assignment" just to get in their door. It would have been easy to get the order by exaggerating the features and benefits to the customers. It would also have been easy to include a few more dollars on the two-day shipping in the delivery cost and not inform them, thinking they would be happier if they received their product sooner.

Sometimes it is not even about lying, but the omission of the truth. And this is absolutely NOT okay!

Although these are easy actions to take and taking them may increase one or two sales, they will not produce long-term results. As a matter of fact, once the customers find out that you were not completely honest with them, you have corrupted everything you have told them about yourself and about your product.

> *People buy because they like and trust you.*
> *When you are a sales rep, you are selling a product.*
> *When you are a leader, you are selling an idea.*

This is exactly the kind of suspect behavior that creates a negative connotation for the sales industry. Many people perceive the "art of selling" as nothing but a group of deceivers who will say or do anything to get your money. The reason some sales people act this way is due to greed and shortsightedness.

These come hand in hand.

Corporate America earlier in this decade has shown us that leaders have often compromised their integrity for personal gain. They went to jail, were removed from their positions, or the companies folded, but all of them lacked integrity.

So understand this - sales and leadership is the same.

People buy because they like and trust you. When you are a sales rep, you are selling a product. When you are a leader, you are selling an idea. Trust is not only gained by merely giving a good first impression but also by keeping your word of what you say you will do. If you are considering lying to your customer about your product or employee about an idea, consider this - maybe your product or idea is just not good enough.

Here are a few ideas to take notice.

First, always do what is right rather than what is easy.

The right thing is never situational. Regardless of what the circumstances, you should deliver what you promise. Dr. Denis Waitley said that "… integrity is like pregnancy. There is no such thing as being almost pregnant. There is no such thing as doing "kind of" the right thing. "

Second, always promise a little and deliver a lot.

Never set a false hope or expectation for the customer or subordinates. No matter how great your product or idea is, it's never as great when you over promise and under deliver.

Lastly, people are always watching.

You will never know whom you are going to work for one day. Regardless of who is watching, the key is that you should do the right things even if nobody is watching. It just makes you feel better about yourself and the work you do.

## Unwavering Vision

Another key characteristic is having an unwavering vision.

I remember the day in my second summer working with Cutco, I came home to my parents and told them that I was going to make $10,000 in the ten weeks of the summer as a college student.

My mom's response was, "You know, your godfather is the head of the Asian Pacific Division of Microsoft. We can get you an internship there."

That could have been the end of my career with Cutco, but I saw people succeed in this business and I kept that picture in my mind. I was not going to let anyone deter me from this vision regardless of current circumstances.

> *Many people have great ideas, but very few people capitalize on them because they don't keep those ideas long enough.*

My parents did not believe that I would be able to succeed. Neither did my friends. They had their reasons not to believe me; the previous summer, I made less than a third of what I was claiming to make the second summer. But my vision of success was so vivid, I had very strong faith in going through with the summer regardless of past results.

I did not make $10,000 dollars that summer as a college student. I made $15,000.

Robert Jarvik, who developed the artificial heart, once said, "Leaders are visionaries with a poorly developed sense of fear and no concept of the odds against them."

How true is this in leadership!

You have to not only create this vivid picture in your mind, but you need to keep it there. Many people have great ideas, but very few people capitalize on it because they don't keep those ideas long enough. A few obstacles and some external influences in perspective can cause them to shift their course.

In sales or leadership, you have to understand that objections and challenges are just a part of the process. Having an unwavering vision helps you develop a sense of purpose - a purpose that gets you so excited that it wakes you up early in the morning and keeps you up late at night. This vision helps to develop an internal drive to achieve your goals in which external motivation no longer seems necessary.

Some call this internal drive passion and others call it enthusiasm. When someone is so excited about where they are going, they tend to attract people with them. People like to surround themselves with those who are excited about where they're going. Enthusiasm is contagious. It moves you and the people around you.

We all have heard that if you don't know where you are going, you may just never get there.

Vision is not simply knowing where you are going, you must also paint a clear picture so you can see it. If your vision is blurry or vague, then it is not a 20/20 crystal clear vision.

One of my favorite questions to ask my organization is "What does winning LOOK like?" A remark of "I want to be successful or I want to be rich" just does not paint the picture for me.

There is a very definite visual as well as feeling associated with where you want to be in the future. It must be so crystal clear that it provides faith when times are tough. It brings out a sense of mission and passion even if you do not know how you will get there.

So really, the unwavering vision really starts with en-vision. Once you commit to a clear vision, the *how* will reveal itself.

## Personal Responsibility

Personal responsibility is another characteristic I am grateful to have learned early in my sales career.

You are able to easily identify the degree of personal responsibility that people take on simply by listening to people's choice of words when they are talking about their work.

I was very fortunate that in every stage of my career, I was able come in contact with many types of people - successful reps and not so successful reps, successful managers and not so successful managers and successful business owners and not so successful business owners. I have found that the degree of a person's success is directly correlated with the degree of personal responsibility a person claims. The more personal responsibility a person takes on for their results, the more successful he tends to be. The more blame a person put on others, the less successful he is.

As a district manager, we often hear reps talk about their results in completely different ways: "My customers are not the type of people that buy" vs. "I just didn't qualify my leads well enough." "The knives are too expensive" vs. "I need to learn to build more value on my presentation."

You can see it on the management level, as well as, when managers say: "My reps are so lazy" vs. "I need to learn to motivate my reps more."

We hear this in business all the time.

"The economy is not doing as well as it was expected and we had a down year" vs "I need to find a way to do better because there are other people doing better than me in the same industry even when the economy is down."

The day that you take personal responsibility for your results is the day that you are really in control of your business. It will be an amazing transformation once you have developed this sense of responsibility. You will look at your business in a completely different way.

It is no longer about how "other people are not good enough" but about "how to make myself better." Taking on personal responsibility has directed me toward personal development. I stopped wishing that things were easier for me. I wished that I were better.

> *If you're in sales, your result is a direct reflection of your effort.*
> *If you are managing people, your people will only be as good as you.*
> *If you are in business, your organization is designed exactly for the*
> *result that it gets*

According to Jim Rohn, "In order for your results to change, you have to change."

If you want complete control of the results you receive, then own it! Good or Bad!

If you're in sales, your result is a direct reflection of your effort. If you are managing people, your people will only be as good as you. If you are in business, your organization is designed exactly for the result that it gets.

When taking personal responsibility for your results, they may not always go in the direction you want. You have to learn that you cannot allow your emotions to take a hold of you. You do not want allow your emotional state to be dictated by your environment.

Rather, you want to become the catalyst for changing your environment. Do not be overly excited for good results and do not be overly distressed over poor results.

Good results are simply lessons of what worked and poor results are lessons of what did not work.

## "Yin and Yang; Body of one." – Book of Tao

### Traits Four, Five and Six

The "Tao" is Nature.

Nature, according to the Taoist philosophy, is governed by the law of *Yin and Yang*. The circle of Yin and Yang is represented by the colors of black and white flows of energy. A white dot in the center of the black energy flow and a black dot in the center of the white energy flow show their intertwining relationship.

Black is female and white is male; black is soft, white is hard; black is negative, white is positive. Taoists believe they must intertwine to reach a level of balance in order for the relationship to work harmoniously in nature.

Just like water, it has the traits of both softness and hardness similar to the idea of Yin and Yang. Water is an excellent representation of the perfect balance; it is hard enough to carve through rocks yet soft enough to seep through the smallest gaps.

Leadership is also governed by this Yin and Yang.

The three characteristics that I have mentioned so far are what I call Yin traits. I categorized them as Yin traits because although integrity, vision and personal responsibility are great leadership character traits, they are not utilized to the fullest without the complement of concrete skills associated with being a leader.

These concrete skills are what I call Yang traits.

In other words, the leader reaches the level of maximum influence only when the specific skills and the character traits are working together in harmony. Just like how the water in the stream is soft yet powerful, your leadership ability will peak when you understand that they are actually inseparable, they exist coherently as one.

The following are the three Yang traits:

## Communication

Communicating is what sales people and business professionals get paid to do.

We get paid to talk. There are two parts to this concept - there are skills associated with communication, but there are also skills associated with getting people to be open to what you have to say.

Through my years of leadership, I have found that the skill of communication is the same in leadership as it is in sales. In sales, I painted pictures for my customers of what it will be like owning the best knives in the world. While leading an organization, I painted pictures of what it will be like achieving their goals.

> *The more people that you can gather around to share your vision, the more momentum you have working toward your goal.*

In sales, I told third person stories of how my customers love the product. As a leader, I told third person stories of other people's success. This provides evidence that other people are doing it, which creates confidence in their decisions, as they are aware that others have already done so.

As a leader, vision needs to be constantly communicated.

When sharing a vision, you are always talking about what is exciting now and what is going to be exciting in the future. For those of you who are leaders, you talk about the bigger picture and you tie it down to what is next for them. This allows them to also own a piece of that vision.

An ancient Chinese proverb says, "When you take one chopstick and bend it with your bare hands, it can be easily broken. When you take a bundle of chopsticks and bend it, it can never be broken." You will lose direction when you do not share your vision. But when you do share your vision with those around you, they serve as a constant reminder and support for you, making it harder for your mindset to diverge.

The more people that you can gather around to share your vision, the more momentum you have working toward your goal. The same is true with selling.

But what makes people want to listen to what you have to say?

I believe it goes back to what we talked about in the beginning: integrity. Can your customers or team trust you? Do you come across as someone who is working with them for their best interests or are you working for your own self-interest?

While the skills of communication are important, it is superficial if people cannot understand your real intention. They don't care how much you know until they know how much you care. Your words are much more powerful when spoken with integrity and with the right intentions.

I once heard that "what you do speaks so loudly that I cannot hear what you say." What you do must be congruent with what you are communicating. Integrity is an inseparable part of effective communication.

## The Skill of Planning And Organization

The skill of planning and organization is another leadership essential.

This is as simple as picking up a planner to plan your sales week schedule and organizing your leads. It is important to have enough analytical skills to predict what to anticipate in the field of your particular business. My ability to analyze and organize was developed and honed by organizing a consistent work schedule as a representative. This later helped me to invent programs that created consistent and uniform results.

Vision without execution is like no vision at all.

In order for you to carry out a vision on the sales or leadership level, you have to bring the vision down to something that is executable. One of the things that I always loved about Cutco is everything is broken down to the ridiculous.

Goals can be easily accomplished when divided into baby steps. Just like breaking down the price of the product to pennies a day, we broke down our goal and vision to the number of phone calls a rep had to make and the number of appointments my team had to do.

When it is broken down, the vision becomes manageable. It is no longer grand. This vision is translated into action steps that are able to bring this vision closer to reality.

Just like a football game, the coach can have a vision and share it with the team by aiming for a specific amount of points they want to score on the board. If that was all the coach had said, however, the players would be directionless regardless of how beautifully he painted his vision. The coach must carry out the vision by assigning individual tasks to each player and providing strategies in different situations according to the play book.

This is what makes a vision complete.

If you fail to plan, you plan to fail. Successful people and businesses always plan to look ahead. By looking ahead, you can anticipate the challenges ahead of time and make educated decisions with the given circumstances.

You may not see all the challenges that will come across due to unforeseen obstacles, but you will be better prepared to handle them. By doing this over and over again, you will soon develop the analytical skills to improve your plans to make future strategic decisions.

Integrity plays a huge role in the execution of your plans. Are you the person that follows your plan? Do you carry out what you say you are going to do? It is never what you said or intended or planned that counts, it is always what you do.

## The Ability To Recruit

The ability to recruit requires someone who can handle the long process of assembling the right team of talent.

The perfect team comes after thorough interviews and interviews managed with the belief that the right one is out there. Persistence is a skill that I have learned as a sales rep through constantly encountering and handling rejections. There are rejections on the phone and on the appointment, but someone will buy as long as I continue with my venture.

Recruiting is a lot like fishing, you just cast and cast and cast because you'll never know when the right one is going to bite. The point is to keep on going until you find the right one for your team.

There is more to it, however, than just having a vision of the team you want to build.

When you recruit the right person, regardless of the task you give them, they might do it well. But the limitation here is you. They may be the right person, but are you?

I once heard, "We don't hire people and train them to be nice, we just hire nice people." So, you must ask yourself, "Are you nice, so that nice people will want to work with you?" That is the crucial question.

I believe that in order for you to attract the right person, you first have to become an attractive person. Earlier we talked about taking personal responsibility and no one else but you can take on the responsibility of developing yourself. Like attracts like and the quality of people that you will attract is dependent upon the quality of you as an individual.

**Knowing others is intelligence; knowing yourself is true wisdom. Mastering others is strength; mastering yourself is true power. If you realize that you have enough, you are truly rich. - The Book of Tao**

Great leaders and entrepreneurs are great sales people.

I have found these six characteristics in the Tao of Selling to be integral when taking on leadership positions. Integrity, vision and personal responsibility shaped my character while the skills to communicate, plan and recruit provided me with tools to execute.

Although these characteristics are divided into the Yin and the Yang, you cannot have one without the other. They are very much interdependent. In a very real way, as much as leadership is about leading those around you, I believe it is much more about knowing yourself and then mastering yourself.

Sales is a great starting point to do just that. Be one with the Tao of Selling and you will see yourself and your organization stand the test of time.

---

**Summary Points**

- Many principles of selling also apply to being a leader.

- Integrity is like pregnancy – there is no such thing as being almost pregnant.

- Having an unwavering vision creates a sense of purpose that wakes you up early in the morning and keeps you up late at night.

- If you want complete control of the results you achieve, then take ownership for 100% of your results.

- In sales, we paint pictures of owning the product for our customers, and as leaders, we paint a picture of future success for our people.

- By looking ahead, you can anticipate challenges and make important decisions.

- In order to attract great people around us, we must become great.

John Edwin is the founder and owner of Strength Personal Training, Inc. Over the past 7 years, he has completed over 13,000 personal training sessions and is one of the premier personal trainers on the East Coast. John also owns L & S Real Estate Development, LLC which purchases, renovates and rents homes in the Philadelphia area. John graduated Cum Laude with a degree in Exercise Science from Liberty University. During his college years, John began working for Cutco Cutlery. He quickly became a top performing salesperson, advanced in the company and went on to run his own Branch office the summer of his junior year. John has won numerous awards for his achievements in sales and customer service.

# Take Your Marks. Get Set. Goal!

## John Edwin

*Nothing happens unless first we dream.*

- Carl Sandburg

It was a hot summer day in June.

I can remember practicing the long jump over and over. I was preparing for an upcoming invitational track meet. My father, who was my coach, was standing next to the sand pit critiquing my steps and encouraging me to jump farther.

After several attempts, my father took out a $20 bill and placed it in the sand. He told me that if I could jump over it, I could have it. I was 13 years old and the first thought that came to my mind was the amount of Snickers bars I could buy with $20.

So, I looked at that $20 bill from the start of the runway and decided to go for it.

My stride was perfect. My jump was perfect and I landed just past that $20 bill! My dad gladly gave me the money and a big hug. He told me that I had just jumped a personal best of over 19 feet.

We took a moment to celebrate that victory. This memory always makes me feel good and that experience became a memorable lesson about goal setting.

Goal setting is one of the most essential aspects of sales. Understanding how to set goals properly will increase your sales production and ultimately, your bottom line. "Practice is the mother of mastery" and goal setting is a skill that we learn and get better at the more we practice it.

Coming out of college, I knew that I was going to go into the field of sales and wanted to someday to run my own business. The four invaluable years that I had spent as a sales rep and sales manager with Cutco Cutlery launched me light years ahead of other recent college graduates.

I had nine job offers with sales companies within my first month of interviewing. I chose to be a sales executive for a Fortune 500 company. But within 5 months I hated the job. I did not feel the support or training was even close to what I had been used to at Cutco.

> *Goal setting is one of the most essential aspects of sales. Understanding how to set goals properly will increase your sales production and ultimately, your bottom line.*

My wife, Christine, recommended that I pursue a career that I would love and be passionate about. So she emailed me an opening to become a personal trainer. I had a degree in exercise physiology and I decided to take the interview.

The fitness manager offered me a job on the spot. He told me they would pay $8 an hour during my shift and $28 an hour during training sessions. The kicker was that each trainer had to find their own clientele.

I laughed and proceeded to tell him that I had a good job with a nice base salary plus commission. The company also provided a company car, an uncapped expense account, a laptop and a cell phone.

"I'm sorry," I said, "$8 an hour does not come close." I left the interview.

A week went by and my wonderful wife told me to leave my high-profile position and pursue a career in the field of health and fitness. She wisely said that since we didn't have children yet, I should take the risk and see where it would lead.

The next day I took the job as a personal trainer.

I was no longer selling something tangible like knives. I now had to sell myself and the vision of how I could help others get healthy. My first goal was to find the top trainer in the company, who conveniently, was working at the same gym. I asked if I could follow him around for a while. No one in the company of over 2000 trainers was coming close to his training volume. So that first week I stuck to him like glue. Since he was 15 years older than me with years of training experience, I picked his brain. I even told him that soon I would be the trainer to compete with him.

His only response was "be careful what you wish for."

I started setting short-term very specific goals for my personal training career. As I hit my goals I continued to adjust them higher and make them harder to achieve. Over the course of the three years that I worked for the fitness company, I was honored to have been chosen as the "Trainer of the Year" all three years.

This award is given to the top 1% of trainers in a company that had over 2,000 trainers working for them. In three short years, I had gone from making $8 an hour to earning well over $100,000 a year.

By my fourth year, I decided to start my own personal training company, Strength Personal Training, Inc. Since my start as a personal trainer in 2001, I have had the privilege to have trained over 13,000 sessions. Some of my clients now pay me over $150 an hour for my training and I am considered one of the premier personal trainers on the East Coast.

Along with my training and God's grace, I now own and operate a rapidly growing real estate company, L & S Real Estate Development, LLC, based in Philadelphia. I am humbly writing this to express that the key to my success is my ability to set goals.

I love sitting down with new clients for a goal setting session.

My first question is always, "Why do you want to start a fitness regime?" Usually, the response is "because I want to lose weight."

My follow up question is, "How much do you want to lose?" The follow up answer is, "As much as possible." Now, that is a goal, but it is not realistic because their answer is not tangible.

There are four key principles which make goal-setting more successful.

> *Give me a stock clerk with a goal and I'll give you*
> *a man who will make history. Give me a man*
> *with no goals and I'll give you a stock clerk.*
>
> - J.C. Penney

## Goals Should Be Challenging And Must Be Written Down

Setting goals that are challenging is my first important principle.

The journey toward a goal, especially when it seems nearly impossible, is where we gain personal growth. Goals force us out of our comfort zone and strengthen us to push our limits. I'm not saying we should set goals that are nearly impossible. But, almost everything great that has been achieved in life, first seemed like a distant possibility. Then, someone considered it, set it as a goal, and began moving towards it. Eventually, even the most challenging goals become realities for someone. Why not you?

Writing down goals is a basic goal setting concept that most people, including salespeople, do not practice. People will tell you that they know their goals in their head. The real reason for not writing down goals is the fear of failure. People are afraid to write down goals because that would mean commitment and if the goal is not achieved, that would be mean failure.

I do not achieve every goal I write down.

But writing down our goals gives us direction. The more you write and re-write your goals, the more you force them into our subconscious mind. Your entire being will be compelled to gravitate toward achieving your goals.

There is power behind writing down your goals.

## Goals Should Be Specific And Time Sensitive

Now that you understand the importance of setting challenging goals and writing them down, it is time to learn to be specific and have deadlines.

A salesperson creating a goal of "selling as much as possible" is not specific.

When you get in your car, do you decide to "drive as far as possible"? Of course not! You get in your car and drive from point A to point B. That is how setting specific goals works. You need to have an exact number of how many deals you want to sell. I would break it down by having an exact sales amount for the month, quarter, half year and year.

Setting your goals with specific numbers in a certain time frame gives you more motivation, and regular feedback as to how you are doing.

By the way, your sales quota is a general goal that your company gives you. I want you to create your own precise goals in order to stretch yourself as a person. Along the way, if your goals are too high or too low, adjust them immediately. You want to be motivated to stay on course.

## Goal Setting In Action

Let me tell you about my friend, Andy.

Andy called me five years ago. He told me that his psychologist recommended him to start setting goals and referred me as his fitness trainer. I set up an initial consultation with Andy to find out how I could help him. Andy came in and told me that he had not gotten on a scale in over a decade.

He recently weighed himself at the University of Pennsylvania and was horrified to see that he was over 400 lbs. He felt that he was killing himself and it was time to take action. Andy was depressed because the doctors at University of Pennsylvania had told him that his only hope was gastric by-pass surgery (This is a MAJOR surgery).

They told him that the most he could expect to lose on a fitness regimen was only 10% of his body weight and there was a strong chance he would just gain it right back. If he did lose the 10% he still would be too heavy to get on a regular scale because they only go up to 350 lbs.

In tears he said he would not subject himself to gastric bypass surgery and that I was his only option. I assured him that he could lose weight and get healthy, but he had to be 100% committed because he was facing a tough road ahead.

> *…Writing down our goals gives us direction.*
> *The more you write and re-write your goals, the more you force them into our subconscious mind.*
> *Your entire being will be compelled to gravitate toward achieving your goals.*

Andy was so de-conditioned that when I first put him on an exercise bike, I didn't even turn the bike on. Not only that, but he made it more challenging by missing three of our first five workouts together.

Since he was so overweight his entire life he could not see himself losing weight and getting "in shape." He literally had to "trick" himself into working out. He made up other reasons for showing up to the gym because Andy could not come to terms with the idea that he was actually there to "work out."

For motivation, we immediately started setting small, specific goals that needed to be hit every two weeks. Gradually, Andy started seeing results. We needed to get past what the doctors had told him. So his first major goal was to lose 10% of his body weight or 40 lbs.

He did this in a few short months. We were walking, slowly, biking, slowly and lifting light weights. I told him that we would gradually need to change his diet and slowly modify his entire life.

We ran into challenge after challenge, but stayed positive by keeping our focus on achieving small, short-term goals.

If I told you Andy's whole story, it would take up this entire book. So, I will abbreviate and tell you that Andy has become a real champion. Over the past 5 years, Andy has lost over 170 lbs. His weight is now in the lower 200s.

Andy now regularly competes in three and six mile races. He is also focused on his first 10 mile race. He was even a guest speaker at a recent fitness retreat. Our ultimate goal is to tell his story on the Oprah Winfrey Show and help inspire hundreds of thousands of Americans to lose weight and live a healthy lifestyle.

Andy has continually set challenging goals. He does write down his goals. His goals are specific and time-sensitive. He approaches them with courage and passion.

## Will Do...Should Do...Could Do...

This concept of goal setting is a slightly more advanced, but relatively simple technique.

The key is to set your goals to three different levels. It does require more time because you're now taking your goals and writing them three different ways. I promise the little extra time invested to follow this method will pay you huge dividends.

The first is the 'Will Do' level. When you are writing out your sales goals, set a number that, if everything goes wrong, is the number you have to hit. Say to yourself, "no matter what, I will hit this goal."

The second is the 'Should Do' level. These goals will be set higher than your "will do" and make you stretch to hit it. Say to yourself, "If things go well, I should hit this goal".

The third is the 'Could Do' level. When setting these goals, I want you to go BIG. At this level, you want to say, "If everything went perfectly, this is what I could do".

Have fun with this one. If you don't have butterflies when writing down these goals, you're not setting them high enough.

*Leaders aren't born; they are made. And they are made just like anything else, through hard work. And that's the price we'll have to pay to achieve that goal, or any goal.*

- Vince Lombardi

## Sales Is The Greatest Profession

I love sales because of its competitiveness.

Winning is a great feeling. Sales companies love to give recognition, trips, bonuses and all kinds of other perks. All you have to do is hit your numbers or win the contests. "To the victor go the spoils".

Good salespeople are always positive, confident and competitive. You need to get very good at setting your goals, not only to compete in the sales field, but also to be the best.

When I sold Cutco Cutlery, I wrote down my goals and placed them where I would see them often, especially when the company was offering trips. I would get travel information and magazines for that destination. I would keep the travel information next to my bed, in my car and in front of me when I made sales calls. This kept me focused on my goal.

When there is not a prize to win, create one. Every time you hit a personal goal, reward yourself. Take a moment to enjoy it. By accomplishing small wins, we eventually look back and take notice that we have accomplished big wins.

I want you to take a moment right now and ask yourself this question, "If success were guaranteed, what goals do I want to accomplish? If everything went my way, how much could I sell this month? If I worked hard and smart, how much could I sell this quarter? If failure was not an option, how much volume could I sell this year?"

Write these numbers down now and remember to be very specific. Give yourself due dates to achieve these goals. Approach your goals with passion and enjoy the journey. Yes, there will be challenges, but remember that in life, most things worth doing are never easy. If you make the harder decisions along the way, you will be successful.

---

## Summary Points

- Practice is the mother of mastery, and goal-setting is a skill that should be practiced and repeated.

- Goals should be challenging and must be written down.

- Goals should be specific and time sensitive.

- The more you write and rewrite your goals, the more they are forced into the subconscious mind.

- If there is not a prize to win, create one and reward yourself for every victory.

- Ask yourself, "If failure were not an option, what would I try to achieve?

- Set goals at different levels: will do, should do, could do.

- Tracking your progress is equally as important as setting a goal and making a plan.

Paulette Renee Tucciarone is New Jersey born and raised. After attending Boston College and then Drexel University, she was accepted to medical school at Uniformed Services University and took her military oath of office in May, 2000. Upon graduation, she moved to San Diego and was deployed twice as her ship's Medical Officer aboard the USS Pearl Harbor (LSD-52). Now back in Washington, DC, she dedicates her professional training to the field of psychiatry, with particular interest in Women's Health and Health Care Politics. Her free time is devoted to time with her husband and family, as well as fitness, reading and the French Horn.

# Dream Me An Objection
# And I'll EQ You Right Out of It

## Paulette Tucciarone

"Sir, we need that helicopter now. I understand there are other challenges in the area and I realize you are looking at other resources, but my patient is losing blood pressure, her white blood cell count is rising and she's been vomiting for the past four hours. We both want her in a hospital on the ground with a surgeon and I need to get her off this ship right now. Do you copy?"

Insert long pause here...

There were some blinking lights in the radio room and all the staff were motionless while they muffled the routine background messages coming through their speakers.

"Copy that, doc. Your bird is on its way."

That was the only sale at which I ever received a round of applause. On the Navy ship where I served two years as the ship's sole physician, in an unnamed area of the vast ocean, I succinctly delivered that objection cycle like I had never done so before.

Few sales closings are as direct as this, and thankfully so, but that day, I made the sale.

In my career as a physician, I've had to make brief, emergency sales presentations and I've had the opportunity to be involved in slow, emotional and painstaking sales. While there are nuances unique to medicine, all these interactions share the same principles I learned years ago as a Cutco sales rep.

I learned the basics and applied them to the advanced lessons. I still employ them every day.

In the days I worked selling Cutco, and even now, I was and am, eager to learn. I had always dreamed of being a physician, from the time I was eight, and learned how to use the microwave for dinner on the long nights my mom spent in the Cardiac Care Unit with my father.

In fact, I went into sales knowing success in medicine would be improved with success in other arenas, and at the bright age of 19, sales seemed a great field to enter. Looking back as I often do, I've realized that I couldn't have been more right.

Of the many lessons I learned selling knives, there are two I keep close to my heart.

The first basic lesson is the objection cycle, which I am guaranteed to use at least once per day. Be it knives, insurance, the trip-of-a-lifetime or medical care, this is a lesson you will want to make automatic in your life, your language and your approach.

When I sit down with a patient today, I jokingly warn them up front that I will not let them object without a fight. They know that I will stay after them, challenge all their objections and hold them to their vows. I believe in my "product." I'm sure they will benefit from walking through treatment in our system and I have the tools to be able to walk through all their objections as necessary.

The second is the most valuable skill set that has been documented in sales research, recruiting, production and duration. It is used by psychics, astronauts, sales representatives and yes, doctors.

It is Emotional Intelligence or EQ.

EQ is a well-balanced tool kit that is rewarding in the toughest of situations and while the space here limits our exploration of all the details, I will tell you where to find its lessons and where I learned them as a beginner. The lessons of EQ can sometimes be complex and challenging, but are well worth your focus. In fact, the essence of these ideas can be best understood through a combination of this chapter and the exercises at the end, so pay special attention to those unique exercises.

When I first began succeeding as a rep, I was your average college student of recently divorced parents, trying to prove my own value to myself and my family and hopefully learning something in the process. I quickly bought into the excitement of my Cutco product and set out to sell "as much as I could."

When I faced those early objections, however, I often folded, not understanding that this was an opportunity to talk even more with my customer, to understand their needs, to appreciate their continuing desire to learn from me.

> *Diplomacy is the art of letting someone else have your way.*
> -Danielle Vare, Italian Diplomat

## The Objection Cycle

The objections I hear to treatment and participation in therapy are many, but they are not that different from the ones I heard as a beginner in sales.

Of course, this is not to say that the concerns my patients provide are without merit. On the contrary, they are often heart-felt, deeply rooted and based in fact. Like most objections, there is always a way to analyze their meaning, discover their source and turn them on their heads. These are potentially life-altering issues and as I see it, all the more reason for me to ensure I manage their objections assertively.

Here are some common objections I hear:

"I understand that therapy can be helpful, but I just don't think I can do it."

"I understand that the DUI looks bad but really, I don't have a problem with alcohol."

"I know this medication can help me, but I think I'll be fine without it."

"I think that my family does care, but I can't face life anymore. It's just too hard."

And here is one of my responses:

Ma'am, I hear you about those side effects and you're absolutely right, they have been reported. However, I think given the severity of your symptoms right now, not acting on them would mean I'm not doing my job. In fact, if you do experience some side effects, I want you to call me right away, because that means the medicine is working and I want to know as soon as possible. So, are you ready to get started with a trial of medication?"

Like any sales person, I have many peers who feel rejected by customers who say the dreaded "no." In psychiatry, we see patients who refuse treatment, who don't show for appointments or who don't participate in therapy. I realize they just haven't bought into our product yet, a product I fully believe in.

I am willing to advertise it and sell it, and more so, I take pride in the moment my patients believe it too.

The fact is, the objection cycle is the same in all kinds of communities - sales, business, engineering and medicine. The same systematic simple language of the objection cycle that I learned selling knives is the trustworthy method I use today.

Here are the four straightforward steps:

1. Acknowledge the customer's objection
2. Provide more information
3. Re-close the sale
4. Be quiet and wait for a response

In my world, the ethical considerations are many, but in most cases, objections are just that – objections - and I make it my job to ensure all my patients are offered the best care. I would not be giving myself the chance to understand my patients if I swayed and I would be remiss if I didn't overcome their objections....or at least give it a throw-down, drag-out, solid try.

> *It is very important to understand that emotional intelligence is not the opposite of intelligence, it is not the triumph of heart over head -- it is the unique intersection of both.*
> -David Caruso

In 2000, I attended my first Tony Robbins conference, "Unleash the Power Within."

I was one of the enthusiastic few who got called to the stage to participate in an exercise about "mirroring." I was to imagine a time of intense emotion, breathe it, see it and without acting, imagine myself in that moment.

Without sharing the moment I was remembering, I closed my eyes and completely dove into my memory, imagining myself walking through the rows of black-gowned college seniors, knowing my name was about to be called. I recalled my internal excitement, the work I put in to arrive at that moment, my times of friendship and times of loneliness, and as I sat in a chair on the stage, my muscles gently tightened and my breathing became more intense.

There was another person from the audience who was called on stage with me and it was her task to listen to my breathing, feel the muscle tension in my arms, look at my body position. Then, she sat in her chair, closed her eyes and mirrored my body language.

In about one minute's time, she could explain what she was feeling: excitement, anticipation, pride, self-confidence, happiness. She didn't have to name the exact event - she could describe my exact feelings by mirroring my behavior.

I was amazed and on that day, I realized that by mirroring people in brief interactions, I could learn, in basic terms, exactly what they were feeling.

I could emotionally meet them where they were on their terms. Understanding people around you is Emotional Intelligence. It's at the heart of our relationships with the people all around us.

This could seem a complex concept for a lot of beginning sales reps.

---

*In those moments, I look at my customer and imagine myself in their shoes. I mirror their behavior. I lean forward when they're upset and they're leaning towards me and I lean back in my chair when they seem uninterested and when they're saying "no." I listen to all my internal emotions. I listen to the words they're speaking and then I listen to what my mirroring is telling me about them. When the time is right, we talk about that together.*

---

How do I emotionally come to understand people and really, how does this help my bottom line? How do I come to understand my customers on a higher level when I am learning how to generate leads and learn the objection cycle and make phone time productive?

I will tell you that gaining EQ is the ultimate goal of anyone interacting with other humans in the business world. Doing it every day you get to practice and incorporate the sales process into your own self.

Anyone who has been a salesperson for any length of time has experienced tough days. We have appointments who don't show, customers who say 'no' and in my case, just insert the word "patients" and we're again talking the same language.

It is tough to feel defeated by phone time and appointment generation, but being aware of our feelings allows us to make, or in some cases not make, the decision to persevere. That experience of self-reflection allows us to build the emotional stability and self-confidence that is a cornerstone of EQ.

The next day, when we choose to re-create phone time with a new lesson in mind, this is a sign of our own motivation and again, can lead to increased self-confidence. This in turn grows into an ability to be less jarred by future challenges from the same experience and therefore subtly teaches each of us to handle increased levels of stress, without feeling stressed.

Looking back on that cycle is the "Ah-hah" satisfaction we search for. It is an awareness of our own growth, and, if we truly develop EQ, it is the same cycle we apply to those around us, seeking to understand and not to judge.

What are the things you can do to reach your full potential? How fast can you feel? Do you, as Goethe suggests, realize your ability to influence the world around you? Can you appreciate, as Herb True of Notre Dame reminds us, that there's a reason therapists charge $150 an hour to listen?

If you're thinking this all comes from some vague economic psycho-babble theories, I can tell you this is not the case. All of these qualities have been measured by corporations as expansive as American Express and the US Air Force, and as small as mom-and-pop corner stores.

These skills translate directly into increased sales, decreased turnover and improved employee and customer satisfaction. They are the qualities that make being social and having "good people skills" actually matter. In learning and practicing everything you do in sales, you are building your EQ, making yourself more marketable and increasing your bottom line.

In the hospitals I work in, I see many patients that are older than me chronologically and also in their understanding of life. They have more experience than I do.

> *There is no CEO worth their salt who does not pay dearly for employees with these skills. In fact, managers pay top dollar for them because in most cases, the individual with high EQ could do the job on their own without that CEO.*

I also see eighteen and nineteen year old soldiers and sailors who already believe I'm too old to understand their needs. We've all been in situations that reflect those seemingly prejudicial scenarios, and in many cases, it's a questionable sharing of power, at best.

In those moments, I look at my customer and imagine myself in their shoes. I mirror their behavior. I lean forward when they're upset and they're leaning towards me and I lean back in my chair when they seem uninterested and when they're saying "no."

I listen to all my internal emotions. I listen to the words they're speaking, and then I listen to what my mirroring is telling me about them. When the time is right, we talk about that together. I handle their objections and I re-close my sale.

This may all seem like a complex interaction, but it starts at the primary sales level. Generating leads, making phone time, presenting products, making mistakes all along the way, being rejected and choosing to happily get back up the next day to do it all over again… that's EQ.

There is no CEO worth his or her salt who does not pay dearly for employees with these skills. In fact, managers pay top dollar for them because in most cases, the individual with high EQ could do the job on their own without that CEO.

I believe succeeding at life's experiences can be likened in some ways to the children's beloved tale of "The Velveteen Rabbit."

In this story, the toys in a child's nursery are well-versed in the fine art of being loved. One of the oldest toys, a bedraggled, one-eyed rocking horse, shares a secret with the newest stuffed creature - a beautiful, lush velveteen rabbit.

In a few well chosen words, he tells the rabbit that "to be really loved, you have to get some of your skin rubbed off..."

This is the exact case with our success in life. Which of us can't remember the "failures" of our greatest leaders?

Here are a few for you to think about:

- Einstein was four years old before he could speak.

- Iassc Newton did poorly in grade school and was considered "unpromising."

- When Thomas Edison was a youngster, his teacher told him he was too stupid to learn anything. He was counseled to go into a field where he might succeed by virtue of his pleasant personality.

- F.W. Woolworth got a job in a dry goods store when he was 21, but his boss would not permit him to wait on customers because he "didn't have enough sense to close a sale."

- Michael Jordan was cut from his high school basketball team.

- Bob Cousy suffered the same fate, but he too is a Hall of Famer.

- A newspaper editor fired Walt Disney because he "lacked imagination and had no original ideas."

- Winston Churchill failed the 6th grade and had to repeat it because he did not complete the tests that were required for promotion.

- Babe Ruth struck out 1,300 times, a major league record.

Vision, self-motivation, emotional maturity…there are countless stories of the personal growth that emerge from a full spirit.

Getting there is the goal. And while they don't all come from starting a sales job as a nineteen year old, that was the experience that helped me gain the skill. The practice of the systematic skills taught in sales is invaluable and has proven to be so in all aspects of my life.

---

## Summary Points

- There will be unexpected times in life when our ability to overcome an objection can have life altering consequences.

- When you believe in your product, it is your job to be as good as possible at handling objections.

- The objection cycle begins with acknowledging the customer's objection.

- When we mirror the physiology of others, we can literally experience what they are experiencing.

- Many of our greatest leaders preceded their successes with multiple failures.

- Being aware of our feelings of defeat gives us a chance to choose to persevere. That experience of self reflection is an example of growing our emotional intelligence.

- Our emotional intelligence allows us to see our challenges as growth opportunities, and therefore experience less stress in our future efforts to overcome obstacles.

John Israel is a member of the Cutco Hall of Fame, as well as a nationally requested speaker on youth empowerment. He performs keynote speeches, workshops and seminars to help young people understand how their current actions today are creating the life they live tomorrow. He also coaches and trains parents about how to create self-reliant youth. You may visit his website: www.johnizzy.com for more information.

# The Midas Touch Of The Salesman
## It's Not About Closing. It's About Prospecting

### John Israel

The story of King Midas is one of my favorites in Greek history.

If you're not familiar with his story, here's the short version: King Midas ruled over a land called Phrygia. One day he found a half-goat half-man creature sleeping on his property. King Midas was merciful and allowed the goat man to go.

Fortunately, that creature happened to belong to the God Dionysus, who then gave King Midas any wish he desired for sparing his goat-man. Knowing that the more money a kingdom has, the more powerful it is, King Midas wished for the ability to turn everything he touched into gold.

Boy did he get his wish!

Trees, chariots, buildings, everything turned to gold.

Unfortunately, King Midas tried to show off the new gift to his daughter, only to turn her into a golden statue. After begging and pleading with the God Phrygia, King Midas was able to get his daughter back as long as he gave up his gift.

That's the end.

There is an underlying theme to this story: be careful what you wish for.

In sales, however, it is said that some people have the Midas Touch when it comes to working with prospects. They seem to find all the "golden" clients. Some call these sales people "lucky"; I call them "good."

> *...a man with people behind him can change the world.*

It's no myth that 80% of business is produced by the top 20% of sales people. That's not just because they work harder, it's because they understand the value of spending as much time in front of the best, most qualified prospects. Every salesperson knows this, but only a small percentage of them do it.

Why?

Simply put, good salespeople get referrals, other salespeople don't.

Aside from breaking records and being a member of the Cutco Hall of Fame, my greatest professional achievement lies in being able to move anywhere in the United States and create a new clientele from scratch (which I did several times). I didn't merely get "lucky." I trained, practiced, and learned from the very best, in and out of my industry.

I learned very early on that the man who knows how to prospect will ALWAYS be in business. Not only will he always be in business, but he will be a leader in that business. Not only will he be a leader in that business, but he will be a leader in the world. Because a man with people behind him can change the world. I still use these principles today as a speaker traveling around to high school and college campuses teaching young people the value of leadership skills.

Having the Midas touch isn't just about having the ability to shake someone's hand and immediately have them open their checkbook. The Midas touch is about having an ability to add such value to an individual that they not only do business with you, but that they want everyone they know to do business with you as well.

I have found three keys to having the Midas touch as a sales person:

1) Create value
2) Create expectations and understanding
3) Create opportunities

The process is very simple, but each step carries immense depth. Like a math equation, if one variable is off, the answer will be also. I have taught this principle all across the country and hear marked results from those who implement the process.

Along with these principles, I will share some of the cardinal sins most sales people make. Let's begin.

## Create Value

There are two things that every salesperson needs to create value in: value in the product or service rendered and value in the salesperson himself.

Every salesperson needs to know, without a shadow of a doubt that it is within the best interest of the prospect to invest in his or her product or service. This comes from having product knowledge and conviction. Product knowledge is simple to attain through training materials and practice. But, don't confuse conviction with mere enthusiasm. I think we have met some salespeople that are so enthusiastic, they can literally scare a prospect away.

Conviction is the unwavering belief that a prospect is making the right decision to own or use a specific product or service. It needs to be genuine.

I remember one of my first sales presentations I had with Cutco. I went to see a neighbor friend who I thought would be nice enough to let me practice my sales presentation. Her name was Mary. Unbeknownst to me, Mary already owned the Cutco product. It happened to be the first "big" purchase she made as a newly-wed over 30 years ago.

To say Mary was enthusiastic would be an understatement. She practically sold me a set of Cutco before I left the house. There was no hesitation to add to her collection. From this appointment on, my career started to flourish. I was sincerely convicted that every prospect should own a set of Cutco and be as happy as good old Mary.

> *Conviction is the unwavering belief that a prospect is*
> *making the right decision to own*
> *or use a specific product or service.*
> *It needs to be genuine.*

Fortunately for a Cutco salesperson, once a client starts using the product, it is almost instant brand loyalty. There is no comparison. However, brand loyalty is great for a company, but "you" loyalty is where the Midas touch begins.

"You" loyalty is where the prospect buys the salesman both during and after the transaction. In his book "The Likeability Factor," Tim Sanders demonstrates how a person's "likeability" is a direct reflection of how well they do in business and in life. Dale Carnegie demonstrated that principle throughout his best selling book "How to Win Friends and Influence People."

People refer who they like because they assume their friends will have the same experience. Everyone wants to do business with those that they like.

They also like the salesperson who is "interested" not "interesting." Salespeople who try to look impressive will very rarely have that impression with their clients. Salespeople who spend time to show a genuine interest in their prospect will forever be in that clients mind.

I once heard "people may not remember your name, they may not remember exactly what you do, but they will always remember how you made them feel."

I remember a client named Cindy from early in my Cutco career. Cindy bought a substantial amount of Cutco but cancelled her order shortly after because she became severely ill and lost her job. Tragic. Most salespeople at this point would give their apologies and tell the client to call them when they are ready to purchase (never to follow up again). I responded a little differently.

---

*Everyone wants to do business with those that they like.*

---

Six months later I sent Cindy a hand written Christmas card offering some words of encouragement and gratitude for getting to meet her. One year later I followed up with Cindy to see how she was doing. She mentioned that the card I had sent meant a lot and that her health was back and so was her job.

What proceeded was nothing short of amazing. Cindy bought what she had originally ordered over a year ago, plus much more. In fact, she bought several times afterwards for the rest of her family. That letter didn't take much time and it didn't require much on my part, but it demonstrated great value for Cindy. The value for her was she was dealing with someone who actually cared for her as a person.

## Create Expectations and Understandings

Once value has been created for a client, it is imperative to understand that they will expect that kind of value from the salesperson every time.

Now Cindy didn't expect me to send her a Christmas card every year, but she did expect me to be consistent with her view of me. I'm a nice guy in general, so it wasn't difficult to maintain that perception with Cindy. Many salespeople, however, have "Dr. Jeckyll/Mr. Hyde Syndrome" when it comes to client relationships.

The salesperson is very nice and says what he needs to say in order to make the sale. Once the sale has been made, all the little promises start to seem less and less important (especially after the commissions have run), leaving the client less than satisfied.

> *A salesperson who is real with his client about what can be expected (whether positive or negative)*
> *and follows through on those expectations, will begin to create that necessary trust.*

I remember a salesman telling me an all too common story. He was finishing with a client and shared with her those wonderful, final words, "If there's anything that I can do to help you further enjoy our product, call me anytime."

As you can imagine, the client followed through on that promise, but the salesman did not. After receiving a few calls from the client, our good old salesman decided to make the follow up call…over a week later! The client was despondent as expected.

It's the little things that show consistency with our clients that begin to build value in our reliability. They will refer clients to those on whom they can rely. A salesperson who is real with his client about what can be expected (whether positive or negative) and follows through on those expectations, will begin to create that necessary trust.

Along with expectations come understanding.

There is an understanding that if what I sell you is everything I made it out to be, you'll refer me to other clients to whom I can offer the same service.

Sounds logical right? Then why are most salespeople struggling to get referrals?

They struggle to get referrals because they struggle to set the expectation for a client to give them referrals. It is perfectly natural for a salesperson to expect referrals. But there is a difference in expectancy and entitlement. Your client will give you referrals through desire not obligation.

It is natural for human beings to desire contributing to each other. It is one of the greatest feelings to know that you made a difference in the life of someone. Believe it or not, your clients want to give you referrals. If you've done the first part right and your clients see value in you and your product, and you have remained consistent, they will be thinking of other people that could use you.

Some will tell you who right away, most will not. It's not that they won't, it's that they don't know how, when, or where. It is the salesperson's responsibility to create referral-generating opportunities for the client.

## Create Opportunities

Let's face it. Humans are natural procrastinators. You do it. I do it (or should I say "don't do it"). That's just a reality.

As a salesperson, the more opportunities you create for a prospect to buy, the more likely they will. The same goes for a client giving you referrals. Typical salespeople close a transaction and assume that the client will call back whenever they're ready to buy or have a referral.

If that's you, don't hold your breath.

Let's look at the reality of that situation. I'm client A. I bought something from you several years ago. There is a very off chance, even if someone I know is in need of your product or service, that I remember your name, how to get a hold of you and if you still exist. And even if I did have all that, psychologically, there are so many hurdles for me, the client, to go through to give you that information.

Psychologically I am no longer a salesperson, but a friend new to their circle of influence.

I learned early in my career that if I continuously did and said a few things in my presentation, my prospects bought 80% of the time. The more prospects I saw, the more sales I would make and the greater my income would become ("This is genius!" I thought as a 19 year old).

So, all I need to do is have enough people to call on to fill my schedule. Since my prospect is of a certain demographic, they most certainly have other friends or connections in that same demographic. Consequently, I decided to alter my presentation so it contained what I needed to say in order to close the sale, but it transformed into a presentation where I became the product.

I turned every sales presentation into a people presentation.

Every rapport-building question I asked (which showed a genuine interest in them and their lives) was catered in a way for them to share with me their circle of influence in the community - friends, family, business associates, neighbors, anyone. The sale would not occur when they bought the knives, but rather when I was referred.

I also didn't discuss leads as "referrals" or "prospective buyers".

I spoke to clients as though their friends were actual human people (which they are). Where most salespeople ask for a referral, I'd simply ask to be introduced. My client would tell me an interesting story about a friend or family member, I'd mention how great they sounded and how I'd love to meet them some time.

Psychologically I am no longer a salesperson, but a friend new to their circle of influence. Ben Gay III, author of "The Closers II", calls this *sales infiltration*. This is being on a level where there is such a synergy with the client that it's not a hiccup to receive a referral. It's just what happens!

But let's not put the carriage before the horse here. I realize in saying these things that not everyone has the possibility of working with a brand like Cutco. How do you get referrals from a sales presentation when you don't have the initial prospects to start with?

I'd be lying if I said it was quick and easy. It is simple, but not easy.

On a 19 year old's budget, I wasn't exactly jumping at the opportunity to spend hundreds and thousands of dollars on advertising. I did it the cheap way. As fun as it sounds, going door to door selling knives is not an ideal job. I spent much of my time prospecting through my circle of influence. Not that there are many college students interested in knives, but their parents and relatives were in my desired demographic.

Also, I joined networking groups such as BNI (Business Networking International). These are great places to develop those initial clients, but – and this is important - these organizations are not designed to just hand people referrals.

> *I spoke to clients as though their friends were actual human people (which they are).*
> *Where most salespeople ask for a referral, I'd simply ask to be introduced. My client would tell me an interesting story about a friend or family member, I'd mention how great they sounded and how I'd love to meet them some time. Psychologically I am no longer a salesperson, but a friend new to their circle of influence.*

The same rules apply to adding value first - both in yourself and your product. They just happen to make the process of referral generating very efficient.

In the blockbuster hit *Boiler Room*, character Jim Young (played by Ben Affleck) referenced the phrase "ABC- Always Be Closing." But I have an addendum to that phrase, "ABP-Always Be Prospecting."

You can be closing all you want, but when the car runs out of gas, it'll be hard enough pulling it out of the garage, let alone getting it onto the freeway. Prospecting all the time allows you to create something from nothing at any time, anywhere, no matter what the market is like. There is always going to be someone, somewhere who needs your product or service.

The best experience I can share about the benefits of the ABP mentality occurred one warm Sunday afternoon in Ventura, CA. I had just walked out of a client's house when I noticed the neighbor standing outside. Being the friendly guy that I am, I walked up to her and inquired about the landscaping job in their yard. Her name was

Christine. I complimented the work so far and introduced myself as "The Cutco Guy."

We talked about the neighborhood, community and different clients I work with in the area. She invited me in for a glass of water and no sooner than me finishing my drink, did she hand over a list of several people I should "meet" in her circle of influence.

But it doesn't stop there.

Christine later "introduced" me to some friends who placed me in a trade show where I could meet literally thousands of potential clients. Long story short, Christine's connections produced over $50,000 in sales that year and continue to do so every year for the company.

Remember this: It's not about being lucky, it's about creating golden opportunities.

---

### Summary Points

- 80% of business sales is produced by the top 20% of sales people.
- Good sales people get good referrals. Others don't.
- A sales person who knows how to prospect will always be in business.
- A man or woman with people behind them can change the world.
- The three keys to prospecting: (1) Create value, (2) Create expectations and understanding and (3) Create opportunities.
- Conviction is the unwavering belief a prospect is making the right decision by buying your product. It needs to be genuine.
- If you promise something to make a sale, make sure you do it. This creates customer loyalty and opportunities for referrals.
- Help your clients create referral-generating opportunities.

- Ask to be introduced, not referred. They are people, not prospects.

- Consistently prospect, in good times and in bad, and you will always be able to create something out of nothing.

- It's not about getting lucky. It's about creating opportunities.

As a college student in the summer of 1994, Adam Stock was the #41 sales rep in the CUTCO world. He was a branch manager and then a district manager for four years. Adam ran a highly profitable district office, helped educate other managers on profitable business strategies and investments and then, joined Merrill Lynch as an investment advisor. Adam currently works for a Fortune 200 financial services firm and heads up the Next Level Planning Group, where he helps clients put the pieces of their financial puzzle together and make optimal financial decisions.

# The Number

## Adam Stock

*The bad news is time flies. The good news is you're the pilot*
-- Michael Altshuler

To prepare for take-off…. Please get a pencil (not a pen… This is important) and use the rest of this page to jot down any mind clutter. That includes any issues or distractions in your business or personal life that will interfere with focusing on this chapter.

Now that your mind is clear, let's begin.

In the box below, write the first number that comes to mind as you answer this question: If you could work only by the hour, how much would you charge?

I have successfully grown two businesses from scratch and currently employ 18 people.

In my 14 years of business experience, I have observed hundreds and hundreds of salespeople and business owners and one thing is crystal clear -- the one factor that separates those who succeed at the highest level from those who don't, is the number you just wrote in the box.

I will refer to the number in the box as "your number."

Your use of your number will determine your success or failure. To ensure failure, continue to do as much work as possible that is less than the worth of your number. This typically includes doing paperwork, making copies, incessantly checking e-mail and voicemail, scheduling appointments, preparing FedEx envelopes to send to clients, sorting your mail, answering your phone when it rings.

---

*Let's agree that in order for you to be successful,*
*you should focus intensely on only doing work that is*
*worth your number.*

---

Before we move on, what if your number is lower than your colleagues?

I've found the phenomenon of "per hour rate" fascinating. How is it that two attorneys can graduate from the identical law school with similar grades, practice similar law and one can end up charging twice as much as another?

This is true with personal coaches, personal organizers, consultants, and many other professionals. Who is determining these rates? Who is setting the fee schedule?

When I've inquired, I always hear "That's what the market will bear."

But I hear that same response from people in the same industry charging dramatically different rates. What's clear to me is that the difference has to do with what each of them, internally, thinks they're worth.

What you think you bring to the table is the determinant. The more value you can bring to your clients, the more you can distinguish what you do from the competition, the greater your confidence will be in raising your number.

The reason I asked you to write your answer in pencil is because you may want to come back and revisit this from time to time. Each year, I've challenged myself to raise my number. I find that as my number increases, I delegate more, refine the activities that I'm working on and grow my business.

Let's agree that in order for you to be successful, you should focus intensely on only doing work that is worth your number. You might even feel a charge of adrenaline just thinking about the idea of never doing any more paperwork or some of the other examples mentioned above. Yowser!

Two years ago, I challenged myself only to work at my number. In those two years my business has grown 42% and 56%.

Here's how you can do it, too: Make a list of all of the activities you can possibly spend time doing in your business. I have done this for my financial planning practice.

After you have completed your list, circle those activities that you'd consider worth your number. How many of these tasks are you doing? If the answer is more than nine, then you are driving your car with one foot on the brake pedal.

So, stop doing those things that are less than your number.

Easier said than done, right?

You might be thinking, "Adam, it would be great if I could just do what I'm best at and get paid a fat hourly rate by a customer or company, *but my world's not that simple!* I don't have the money to hire enough other people so that I can just focus on selling. It would be great if all I did was sit in front of clients and prospects. But if I did that, nothing else would get done—paperwork, proposals, scheduling, etc.. At the end of the day, I need to do X hours of less than my number work in order to get paid for Y hours at my number."

Delegation is what separates the highly successful from those who don't achieve success. It is possible and you can make it happen.

Here's how to stop doing all of the things that are less than your number:

1. You need someone else to do the less than your number things instead of you. This means hiring and paying someone and providing effective training.
2. You need the confidence that, by hiring someone else, you will be able to fill the freed up time with more your number activities.

Do you think to yourself: "If I only had more time to call and see all of my referrals…" ?

Then it's easy to have confidence that you will be able to fill the freed up time with more your number activities.

What if you don't have lists and lists of referrals to call? What if you're unsure that you'll be able to fill the freed up time with more your number activities?

A client of mine emigrated to the U.S. from Russia in the early 80s with $400. Twenty-five years later he is a self-made millionaire with a thriving computer company. His favorite Russian saying is "He who does not risk, does not drink champagne."

Hiring someone is always a risk. In order to gain confidence with the risk of hiring someone to do the less than your number tasks, first recognize that the majority of your number tasks involve creating new business. Then, work diligently to improve your referral gathering and marketing plan.

Finally, look at the worst outcome - you'll hire someone to do the less than your number tasks and you won't find enough your number tasks to do. You will let the person go, having spent a couple thousand dollars and you will revert to where you were before.

> *Delegation is what separates the highly successful from those who don't achieve success.*
> *It is possible and you can make it happen.*

From experience, I can tell you that this is not a likely outcome. Why? Because hiring someone to do the less than your number tasks will force you to focus on your number tasks. You will be handsomely rewarded for that investment many times over.

So, as the Buddhist saying goes: "Leap... and the net will appear."

Now, look back at the complete list of activities you can do in your business. It's easy to get bogged down in these activities. Or, you can delegate.

Sink your spirit and soul into this concept - if you delegate everything on your list of activities that are worth less than your number, your profits will soar. You will feel a greater sense of control over your destiny. You will feel like you have gotten out of first gear and are shifting into higher and higher gears, ultimately accelerating on the expressway with much less effort.

So, how exactly do you get out of first gear?

## The Four Fears of Delegation

I've learned by working with business owners and professionals over the last 10 years that the four fears preventing delegation are:

1. The person to whom you are delegating can't do it as fast.
2. The person to whom you are delegating can't do it as well.
3. You are concerned about what might happen if the person to whom you are delegating doesn't execute properly.
4. You feel that, by asking people you hire to do menial tasks, you will come across as "better than" or cocky and you aren't comfortable with being perceived that way. So, you end up doing a lot of busy work yourself.

Let's go through each of these:

## Fear Number One: You feel you can do it faster than the person to whom you are delegating

Of course you can. Should we just move on to number two?

No, of course not. The idea is not that you can take 30 minutes to do something that would take someone else 45 minutes. That's almost always true. The idea is simply one of economics and mathematics.

It's easy to know the value of your employee's time because you probably pay him or her. So, if your number is $100, then the opportunity cost of doing this 30-minute project for you is $50. If you are delegating the project to someone earning $40,000 a year, this equates to roughly $20 per hour ($40,000 ÷ 2000 hours). Therefore delegating the same project to your $20 per hour employee (even though it takes them longer) is going to cost you $15. The economic difference between the cost of you doing the project ($50) and your employee ($15) amounts to $35 more to you.

Now imagine what happens when your number is twice as much, yet you're still paying your employee $40,000 per year. Now, the economic difference between the cost of you doing the project ($100) and your employee ($15) is $85 to you.

The emotional difference can also be tremendous if you, like me, get bothered, irritable or emotionally drained by doing tasks that you feel others could or should be doing. Bottom line - by delegating to those whose number is less than yours, you continue to do your number activities.

I mentioned at the beginning of this chapter about professionals doing un-professional tasks. The reason why this happens takes some soul-searching. Many people don't delegate because the task-y things they are doing are distractors -- happily preventing them from doing what is more difficult, yet more profitable work.

For example, making phone calls to prospective clients can be highly profitable work, but uncomfortable work. Therefore, you may find yourself doing lots of other things and justifying them as "important" such as checking e-mail, filling out forms, generating proposals or hole-punching reports.

Rather than organizing your appointments in one area, do you waste time driving excessively from one appointment to another?

There are plenty of other distractors that are hard to justify as work-related, but you may spend time doing them anyway. What are your enjoyment distractors? Looking at Facebook or MySpace, talking to co-workers, taking a long lunch, watching TV, playing with your Nintendo Wii?

All of these distractors prevent you from doing your number work, reduce your productivity, and ultimately cost you enormous amounts of money. Now, in the box below make a list of all of your distractors.

Distractors aren't listed as an expense on a monthly profit/loss report. However, they are expenses. Everything other than key focus activities is an expense.

It's not only what you do that matters, it's how you do it. For example, if you take time to plan your day, time block, organize the leads you're going to call, etc., then you are creating more time to do your number activities.

If you are disorganized, then you will spend much more time thumbing through papers, flipping through leads sheets, getting directions, getting lost, and wasting your number hours.

Have you ever gone home after working a long day and feel that you've done a lot?

If you aren't completely honest with yourself, and continue to fill your day with distractors, you will likely become depressed. You'll feel like you are working too hard for what you're accomplishing.

A reminder: it's not the number of hours that matter, it's the number of hours you spend doing your number activities.

## Fear Number Two: You think you can do it better than the person to whom you are delegating

You almost always can.

Remind yourself what your number is. Now, commit to asking yourself, "Is what I'm doing now a my number per hour job?" If it is less than your number, then even if you can do it better, you need to delegate it.

Often times, we need to apply the old carpenter's adage of "measure twice, cut once." Effective delegation means showing someone else how you do something, instructing them as you do it, watching the person to whom you are delegating do it and then letting them do it without your guidance.

This is how to gain confidence that the craftsmanship or quality of the work will be to your satisfaction.

As the next story illustrates, some activities don't need your precision.

My wife Melinda and I share many of the household chores. I like folding laundry more than she does and she likes doing some other chores more than I do. I always fold my shirts and socks in a particular way.

When Melinda folds laundry, she folds the shirts a different way and puts the socks in a ball. As you have more life experiences, you learn not to make such a big deal out of these things, but the way Melinda folds shirts and socks used to make me batty.

So much so, that on the couple occasions that she folded laundry, I would unfold my shirts, un-ball my socks, and do them the way I like them.

Bonehead Move #1. Did I thank Melinda for taking the time to fold the laundry? No.

Bonehead Move #2. What was I saying by re-folding my laundry? I was saying, "Not only am I not thankful to you, but you spent your time doing it wrong and I'm going to spend more time doing it right."

Bonehead Move #3. I was ultimately saying to Melinda, "Don't ever fold the laundry again."

Bonehead Moves #4, 5, and 6. Aside from the rough start, the ending to this story is a happy one. We stopped acting stubborn. When I fold the laundry, I now fold my things the way I like them, and I put her socks in a ball.

The Platinum Rule: Do unto others as they would have you do unto them.

The business application of this household story is: When you scratch beneath the surface, are some of your business tasks like folding shirts or socks? Do they really need your precision? If they come out slightly different, will that be okay? Might they even be better?

**Fear Number Three: You are concerned about what might happen if the person to whom you are delegating doesn't execute properly.**
Many people see this as the problem, when it is truly a symptom of a much bigger problem—your hiring and firing practices.

You will find that the better you are at hiring quality people, getting the right people "on the bus" as author Jim Collins describes it, the more trust you will have in their performance. If you cut corners in your hiring approach or offer a wage that attracts a lower talent pool, then you are inviting future frustration.

Here's a great way to instill confidence in your new hires: Let them know that for the first couple of months you will be micro-managing them to make sure that they learn the systems and processes precisely. This will improve their confidence and will ultimately lead to you give them even more responsibility.

We feel like we are wasting time by showing, instructing and watching when we could just do it ourselves. In the end, we save a lot of time.

**Fear Number Four: You feel that, by asking your employees to do less than your number tasks, you will come across as "better than" or cocky. You aren't comfortable with being perceived that way. So, you end up doing a lot of busy work yourself.**
This fear is very common and I suffered with this fear for a large part of my early business career. This is a sample conversation of how I have managed to overcome it, through open, honest communication:

> Pat, there is nothing that anyone does in this business that I view as "beneath me." I am willing to roll up my sleeves if necessary, come in on the weekends and help if you or anyone else feels overwhelmed with their work. Pat, everyone's job who works here is to help me stay focused on the activities that I am best suited for. When this happens, our organization makes more money and everyone ultimately gets paid more. You can help in two ways.

First, if you see me actually doing things that you think aren't the best use of my time, can you please offer to do them? Also, if you look ahead and see things that might distract me, can you please take care of them? Are you okay with that responsibility?

Since everyone shares the your number model, they see their contribution as part of a bigger whole.

Okay, ready to make the number work for you? Try this exercise:

1. Look back at the number in the box. What would you need to do to double your number?

2. You may be able to answer this question by first answering some other questions:
   a. In what areas am I lacking as a professional? Appearance? Poise? Technical Skills? Speaking? Listening?
   b. Who do I know whose number might be double my number? What do they have that I currently don't possess and how might I grow that?
   c. What learning courses, books, audio CDs, etc. are available to me to grow my talents, skills, and ultimately my confidence?

3. Are you earning your number-type money? Here are some estimates for how much you *will make* this year if you work 40 hours per week, 48 weeks per year, earning your number:

   If your number is $25, you will earn $48,000 this year.
   If your number is $100, you will earn $192,000 this year.
   If your number is $250, you will earn $480,000 this year.
   If your number is $525, you will earn $1,008,000 this year.

4. So, how far off were you last year from your number? How much did you *actually* make per hour? The above equations give you a benchmark against which to measure your ability to master the information in this chapter.

**Summary Points**

- The more value you can bring to your clients, the greater your confidence in your personal worth.

- The most valuable tasks for you are likely those that involve creating new business.

- Stop doing those things that another can do for less than your time is worth.

- Hiring someone to do your less valuable tasks will force you to focus on your most valuable tasks.

- Fears that others won't be able to do your tasks as fast or as well as you can are natural, but don't justify doing everything yourself.

- Improve delegation by letting your staff know that you will be working closely to make sure that they learn the systems and processes precisely.

- Teach your team that when they succeed at their tasks, it frees you up to bring in more revenue, which is good for everybody.

Jason Bennett Scheckner was born in raised outside of Philadelphia, PA. He attended Franklin & Marshall, where he studied Business Management. He began working for Vector Marketing / Cutco Cutlery in college and upon graduation pursued a management role in Providence, RI until the end of 2004. Jason then spent the next three years as a Sr. Account Executive with DHL Express. In 2007 he was ranked nationally in the Top Three Representatives. He currently works as the Sales Director for BountyJobs.com, an internet startup in New York City.

# Boardroom Sales Strategy
# I Learned at the Kitchen Table

## Jason Scheckner

I am sitting across the table from an executive-level decision-maker with a million dollar deal at stake and it is up to me to win the business.

This is my idea of the dream sales call.

Today I revel at the opportunity for challenges like this and find them completely non-intimidating. I sometimes wondered how I had overcome the intimidation that accompanies this sort of accomplishment. I realized upon evaluation that it was my sales approach that allowed me to add value beyond the client's expectations.

This selling style, also known as "Consultative Selling" can enable anyone to succeed under the boardroom lights.

Learning the consultative sales approach took me more than eight years to master. My hope is for current and aspiring sales professionals to benefit from the lessons I explore in this chapter and put the basics into practice today.

While working with Cutco Cutlery from 1998 through 2004, I began to expand upon traditional sales methods and approach sales using a consultative method instead. I had no idea while sitting down to demonstrate a set of cutlery at my neighbor's kitchen table that I was laying the foundation for the consultative approach that I use today. This consultative method enables the client to make informed decisions to buy, without using forceful tactics, and is thus more comfortable for both the client and sales person.

I cannot take credit for the consultative method, but I will relate how I arrived at the consultative sale naturally, and why it has been the most powerful concept I have applied in accelerating my sales growth over the years. If you implement the two consultative strategies described herein you will experience the following dramatic changes. You will:

- Be able to identify a customer's true needs and provide a compelling recommendation and solve a problem.

- You will feel more confident about presenting your material because it will be relevant to each specific customer.

- You will not be stricken with anxiety when it comes time to ask for the order.

- You will feel a more fulfilling sense of achievement following the sale as opposed to potential remorse.

- You will become more confident in the value you provide to your clients thereby increasing your closing ratio.

My closing ratio consistently averages at eighty percent. This is a direct result of the techniques I learned while selling knives and later sharpened while executing high-level sales calls. I encourage you to learn from my discovery and let go of conventional sales methods.

My goal for you is to approach your work as a business consultant, rather than as a sales representative.

## Awakening the consultant within

Today, I am passionate about my career in sales and wouldn't change a thing about how I arrived where I am now. I will share with you that I did not always want to be a sales professional. Imagine that!

When I started my freshman year at Franklin & Marshall College, I was enrolled in the pre-healing program. I was going to be a doctor. Many of the reasons I wanted to be a doctor are also the reasons I approach the sales process the way I do.

Doctors spend their appointments solving problems, so it is no surprise that I was drawn to a consultative approach. Business consultants also solve problems. They look for resolutions to concerns, like how to improve processes, how to maximize efficiency, and how to reduce costs.

After my first summer selling knives, I spent many years with Cutco as a Sales Manager. When the day comes that you are asked to explain and teach others your own methods, you actually start to recognize certain strategies and techniques that are a natural part of your success.

I encourage you, for this reason, to train your peers.

This will be an immensely rewarding chance to understand how and why you approach your sales appointments the way you do. It was while teaching others that I began to categorize techniques of the consultative method.

After Cutco, I transitioned into a business-to-business sales role. I spent 3 years as an account manager with a worldwide logistics and transportation company. My customers were shipping and office managers, directors of procurement, VPs of Logistics, CFOs, and even Presidents. In this role, I was finally able to put a name to the process that I had grown into over the years. I was able to define the techniques that I will share with you in the context of the consultative sale and put these techniques to work in the boardroom.

I used the refined consultative methods to propel myself to success. I was able to land multiple contracts in excess of one million dollars that required boardroom level execution, ranking in the top three nationally among all my peers.

## A Traditional Foundation

When you first learn sales, you spend a lot of time learning traditional approaches that are proven to work regardless of skill, in order to produce a consistent closing percentage. These "traditional" sales methodologies want you to follow the script and memorize the close, asking for the sale.

I do agree that a good script is effective because it is designed to answer the question "why should I buy?" for the average customer, and the goal of closing is to review the reasons to buy and to finally ask for the sale. There is nothing wrong with doing this, as it allows you to become familiar with the product or service and the nuances of presenting it to a client. Most importantly it allows an inexperienced sales person to grow comfortable asking a customer to buy.

I will emphasize that you need to know your script inside and out before you attempt to implement consultative selling methods because the consultative sale is the natural evolution of the traditional sale.

I noticed that as I began to evolve that there were two overwhelming feelings that began to awaken the consultant within.

- **The same material doesn't work for every call**: I became bored presenting the same material, the same way, everyday.

- **Closing felt uncomfortable and insincere**: I felt awkward at the end of the presentation when I had to ask a customer to buy in a scripted way.

These feelings had nothing to do with whether or not I thought the customer should buy. I truly believed that every client should own the products I represented.

If you represent a good quality product or service and you feel this way, it won't be an issue.

My drive was to make my client feel more comfortable with the sale. I noticed when I began to use rudimentary forms of the consultative sale and catered the call to the client, that my percentage of sales increased and I didn't get the nervous knot in my stomach when I asked them to buy. This is because, in contrast to traditional methods, the consultative approach requires you to set your intentions about the approach in advance.

The lesson here is that the subject matter that you cover with your client and the order in which you deliver this information, depend on the customer.

My goal for you is to be able to quickly and consciously apply the techniques of the consultative sale. This process has many techniques which will redefine the way you approach each sales call. I will share two of the most basic and powerful techniques.

## 1. Listen, Ask and Align

The first strategy of the consultative sale is to listen, absorb, and use the information you gather to present your product or service to the customer. This is how you identify the customer needs and align your product with those

**I remind you of this oldie, but goody-** "You can't listen to what the customer needs with your mouth open."

## a. Listening in order to learn

In order to find out what is important to your customer, you must listen.

If you can execute the practice of listening, you will see immediate results, because you are adhering to two basic principles of human interaction.

One is that people much prefer to talk about themselves rather than listen to you.

And two, most people don't have the attention span or more importantly, the motivation to listen to most sales presentations.

It can often feel like "information overload" to the customer. They cannot retain everything you cover, so focus on what matters. Also, I found when I didn't say as much, people listened more when I did speak.

If you do more than fifty percent of the speaking during a consultative sales appointment than you have done something wrong.

Think of a true business consultant. In most cases their job is to analyze a company by conducting thorough research and information gathering. It is not until that data has been processed, correlated, and evaluated that the consultant makes any recommendations.

You need to think about your appointment as an information gathering exercise, which will require you to process the information you gather to be presented later as a recommendation.

## b. A lot of telling is not always the key to a lot of selling.

You can build on the skill of listening by understanding when you should do the talking in an appointment.

Don't underestimate the difficulty of restraining yourself from speaking too much. One of the fundamentals that separate the consultative sales call from a traditional sales call is that it is not unilateral. In a traditional sales call, the goal is to cover everything and hope that something sticks. Basically you are inundating the customer with as much information about your product as possible.

Let me give you an example. In a Cutco demonstration, we used to say, "Most people have a drawer full of knives that are broken, don't match, and most importantly, don't work properly." We would then proceed to identify every single problem with common knives, such as the unsanitary qualities of wooden handles, the poor longevity of plastic handles, and the utter danger of the partial tang (this is how far the actual metal goes into the handle).

These are in fact all very true statements regarding the average American household's kitchen drawer.

This is called the shotgun approach - try and hit everything. We are doing the telling and even worse, we are potentially telling them something they don't need to know. For example, what if they don't own any wooden knives or what if more importantly they don't have inexpensive knives, but instead they own a high quality set.

If that is the case, then the entire section on the problems with cheap knives becomes trivial and extraneous.

The author T.S Eliot said, "If I had more time, I would have written a shorter letter."

This quote reminds me of the consultative approach. If you think more about your presentation and your audience, you can say far less and communicate more.

So, by now you may be asking yourself, "If I am not going to tell them what is wrong, what am I supposed to do? Have them tell me what is wrong?"

The answer is absolutely yes. I'll show you how.

## c. Ask and ye shall receive

People love to talk.

So you may ask, "Why don't some customers just tell us what their concerns are so we can solve them?"

The reason is simple. Another human instinct is overriding all other impulses. The prevailing instinct is one of the most basic of all species, which is to protect itself. People naturally perceive sales calls many times as an "intrusion" both physically and mentally, which is consistent with many of the stereotypes about sales.

I encountered a great example of this perception in my current job. I work for an internet technology company called BountyJobs, that offers a website which connects employers and search firms. There is no cost for a client to use our site. In fact the client incurs zero incremental costs to use our service and is likely to save "soft" costs related to increased efficiency and streamlined processes. Our website offers our clients a tremendous value proposition with zero downside to even just trail the service.

Surprisingly, I still find clients putting up barriers. I often think to myself "Did you hear me say this doesn't cost anything?". This defense mechanism is a natural manifestation of their need to defend and protect themselves, to resist change. Their guard is up before I even present the product, and the same is true of your customers.

Now that you know people are not forthcoming with all their reasons to buy, it is imperative to obtain this information. The simplest way to get what you need from the customer is just to ask.

So, in the traditional telling example above, you just restructure the statement as a question. "Most people have a drawer full of junk knives, so what are some of the common problems you have with the utensils that you use?"

The next step is to be quiet and let them tell you. Be careful! This is one of the most common areas where I see representatives make a terrible error. They ask poignant discovery questions and before the client can give an answer, they interrupt with what they assume the answer might be. Just be patient and remember to listen.

When the customer tells you their problem, this is a huge step. For instance, if they tell you they have a whole set of old grimy wooden handled knives; you have learned that you can now elaborate on the problems with wood handles.

The value of this information is that you don't have to spend time discussing problems which are not relevant to them.

### d. "Is this where it hurts?"

Just like a doctor uses the information the patient tells him to make a diagnosis, so must the consultative sales person.

Sometimes the patient isn't obvious either, so you need to ask probing questions. For example "Does it hurt when I do this?" What you are looking for are pain points. These are areas of discomfort that you can fix with your product or service.

It is critical to keep your ears open for opportunities to uncover pain points below the surface too. Sometimes the reasons to buy aren't always obvious. You might ask a question and their answer might not be too revealing. In this case you need to explore the initial answer.

For example, you ask the customer "If you could have the perfect set of knives, what features would you want them to have?"

If their answer is "I want them to stay sharp," you can actually dig deeper to focus on the pain point. You have to find the painful experiences of the customer or there is no value to buy.

You might say, "If they don't stay sharp, what does that mean to you?" Typically they might say, "Well I have to sharpen them all the time, which is inconvenient and takes a lot of my time and if they are dull I could really injure myself."

In my current role, I often ask clients, "If you aren't able to fill this position in a timely manner, how does that impact the company?" I like to follow up by asking "How does this affect you?" This makes the pain very personal.

By following these practices, you have identified genuine problem areas. You've just learned, going back to our doctor metaphor, that they have a broken hand and you are pressing on it; "Oh, so it does hurt when I do that?" You lead them to that realization by asking directing questions.

Watch out! The time to offer your remedy in the form of your product's benefits is not always immediately when a wound is discovered. We need to understand the whole picture before we offer a diagnosis. Your appointment is initially about research and information gathering.

This can actually be an appointment, in and of itself, often referred to as a discovery call where we just learn about the need and we setup a second call to offer the solution once we have had time to understand the client's true needs.

When the time does come to sell the benefits of your product, that's when you laser focus in on the benefits which solve the problem. More importantly you align these solutions with your product.

You've cut out the problems they don't have. You've gotten rid of the benefits that don't matter to them and now, you can show them how your product can solve their problems. In the traditional approach, it's like the patient was diagnosed with a skin condition and the doctor spent time telling the patient about concerns and ways to prevent heart disease.

Certainly useful info, but it's not the problem. You can apply this general investigative technique to any product and service. When you do, your diagnosis will be more openly received. This is especially important if your discovery reveals something that the client may be embarrassed or shocked to have learned during your call.

### e. Agreements are the key to a sale.

When I refer to agreements, I don't mean signed legal contracts. I mean conscious affirmation on the part of the customer.

The latter has the same affect as the former which is that it gets the customer to commit. Make sure when you offer solutions to your customer, you do so in the form of a leading question, not a statement.

For example, "You mentioned that you can't stand unsanitary products and with three kids in the house, that safety is a huge concern. If you could have a product that eliminated those issues would you be interested?"

They say, "Of course." Congratulations, you have accomplished something very important here. They just agreed with you. This is a fantastic approach I learned selling knives. Let me show you how I applied it at the corporate level.

"Mr. Vice President, you mentioned that when your samples arrive late from China, this can seriously affect your ability to get your product to market. So, if you had a way to ensure your goods would arrive, including customs clearance, exactly one day after they were picked up from your factory overseas, would you be interested?"

Mr. Vice President says, "Of course."

"Mrs. Director, you mentioned that having to negotiate contracts with thirty different head hunting firms each year can be grueling and that your lack of visibility to search activity across the organization is extremely concerning. So, if you had a way to consolidate your contracts through one vendor, while gaining access to monthly and year-to-date reports at no additional cost, would your company be interested?"

Mrs. Director says, "Absolutely."

Look for areas in your own sales approach where you can describe benefits in the form of a question. This helps you get your customer to say "Yes," not in a tricky way, but in a manner that justifies the solution.

This first technique will help you build a case throughout the presentation and when you get to the summation, the jury has already made up their mind about the verdict.

### f. Point to the "Get" while you get to the point.

The consultative sale is about narrowing in on the solution that is relevant to your client. Your goal is to find at least one problem and align your product with the solution.

When it comes time to offer your solution make sure you "Point to the Get." In other words, summarize the problems and explain how you will solve those.

Here is an example, "You mentioned today that you would like a set of knives that didn't take so much time to sharpen and didn't make you nervous around the kids and that they were the right tools to accomplish the right task, so you wouldn't risk injuring yourself...Let me show you how we solved that problem." At this point the benefits of your product as a solution are entirely meaningful because you have helped the client understand the problems.

### g. The best salesperson at every meeting is your client

If you can get your customer to tell you why they should by, then you have accomplished three things. You have uncovered a why to buy. You have gotten them to tell themselves the why. And you have eliminated all the unnecessary information that doesn't pertain to them.

One of the best pieces of sales advice I can offer is to let a client figure out and say out loud why they need your product. You just need to help them in that discovery process.

### 2. For And With

The second consultative strategy will help you feel at ease when it comes time to ask for the sale.

The strategy can be defined by the answer to this question, "When you make a sale, is it something you do to the customer or for and with the customer?"

The answer defines how you sell. If you answered "for and with," then this chapter is for you. If you answered "to," then this chapter is definitely for you.

When you sell "for" the customer you are ultimately answering the question for them "Why should I buy?" You are presenting the rationale that corresponds directly with their desires and needs. If you do your job to help them arrive at the "why," the rest is just logistics of when.

## a. The right reasons lead to the right results

One interesting realization which is especially true for unseasoned sales people is that it is very important to know why the customer wants to buy.

This makes it much easier for you to ask for the sale. Here's the bottom line - regardless of how you arrive at the why, if you don't ask someone to buy, most people just won't do it themselves.

If you know you've set out to help the customer make a decision on their behalf, you won't hesitate to help them buy your product, especially when it is very clear why they should buy. Sometimes it actually feels more like you are giving good advice backed up by all of the information you learned from the first technique.

This style is about how you fundamentally approach the selling process. What can I offer that can genuinely help the customer? You will end up with a satisfied and happy client, if the entire call/appointment aligns itself with that goal.

## b. Be a Team Player

The first tip I can give you toward implementing this technique is to consider yourself a part of the customer's team.

This helps to build up their confidence to override the "protection" instinct that we discussed earlier. What would be the impact of the decision to go with your product or service if you worked for their company or you were a member of their household?

It boils down to this concept - you win when you want your customers to win first.

This aligns with how many business consultants are compensated – they are paid based on the amount their customer saves as a result of their recommendation. They have a vested interest in their customer's success.

When I was an account executive for the transportation company, I liked to think of myself as an extension of the customer's logistics team. I made recommendations based on how it would affect not only their bottom line, but their people and processes.

This is where the consultative sale can be a huge win.

When I was able to save customers money and improve their process, I felt great about that. I had pride in their success. I felt like what I offered them truly improved their current situation. You want to make them feel good about how your product or service will be a great change for them. You don't need to make people feel bad that what they are doing is wrong, or life will end if they don't change.

Let's face it; before you got there they were getting along.

Apply this to a direct sale in the customer's home, too. Think of yourself as part of their household. When you make recommendation think how it will affect their team and process. A great example is when you are selling to one spouse and you lose the sale when the other spouse returns home. The way around this – you must address how the other spouse is represented in your presentation.

One of my favorite boardroom stories involves an extremely successful e-commerce company called Amazing Clubs. Their business offers various "amazing" products in an "of the month" offering, such as wine, beer, cookies, flowers, etc.

When I sat down with them, they were growing at a tremendous rate. My goal was to win their monthly distribution portfolio. The deal was worth well over a million dollars a year and they were growing at about 100% a year.

When I first sat down with them, I knew they had already tried my company in a trial and experienced undesirable results. They were very happy with their current providers. Before I even sat down to talk with the CFO to tell him what I could do for them, I knew I was already selling against a bad experience, a happy customer and a bevy of demands.

I'll never forget the meeting where the team player concept came to life.

I was meeting with the client to present our proposal. At this point I had followed the consultative strategy to present the solutions we had customized for the client. The issue was that our proposal was cheaper in some areas for the client but far more expensive for them to ship certain products, especially as it pertained to geographic origin and destination pairings. The issue was that there was no net benefit for the client to switch from their current provider.

We were sitting around the conference table with the CFO. The CEO and CMO happened to walk in during the appointment. The pressure was on! Having worked hard to understand the customer's portfolio of business a moment of clarity occurred.

"What if we got creative?"

I proceeded to explain to the customer that we could approach the proposal differently, because we had more flexibility on our over-night pricing margins than our standard ground services.

Since we had always been comparing apples to apples it never occurred to me, but if we converted their shipments to over-night we could actually lower costs based on the origin of the shipments and at the same time provide their customers with a faster delivery time.

When I finished, I remember the rush, not from knowing that I had probably guaranteed the sale, but in knowing that I had helped the client's business.

I continued to "own" the sale by visiting the client's warehouse, over three hours away, to ensure our hardware systems were properly installed and integrated. I customized a claims process to help eliminate hassles related to damaged and broken goods, and I continued to visit the client regularly to monitor the progress.

I used the consultative approach and took personal pride in the success of my customer. I knew that shipping was a huge portion of their operating costs and therefore had a huge impact on their business. If I didn't care about the customer's success in this case, I don't think this sale would have ever happened. I am sure the customer knows that I cared because we still keep in touch today, even now that I no longer work for their strategic vendor.

They invited my wife and I to their summer and holiday parties. I was the only non-employee invited to attend.

## c. If you can add value, they will value your opinion.

Don't be afraid to make recommendations. You've probably earned their respect and their ear during your presentation. Be sincere in your recommendation. The client is buying you as much as they are buying the product.

Insincerity is painfully obvious.

Here is an example of a strong recommendation.

"Based on some of the problems you mentioned to me today, I can genuinely tell you care about making the process easier for your people, and I can honestly say this product will do that for you. I would recommend starting with a 2 week trial… this will give you factual information to justify your decision to change, as well as, help your people build a comfort level with our service. Assuming the trial goes smoothly, and I know it will, we can discuss a full implementation plan that fits a timeline you are comfortable with. How does that sound?"

Beware. When you find a solution that makes a sale, it's easy to recommend that same solution to all clients, but you are missing the whole goal of the consultative sale. Just like a presentation can be canned, so can consultative recommendations.

The best part about the consultative sale is that you barely have to ask for the sale

Just summarize the information you've collected along the way.

"So, today you mentioned our solution will save your people time, allow you to cut out unnecessary overtime hours, leverage your spending power and give you reporting that allows you to manage your people."

And all you have left to say is, "When can we get you started?"

See, I told you that would feel more comfortable.

Whether you are sitting at the kitchen table or the conference table, the customer needs must be met. I wouldn't have the confidence I have today to comfortably ask for a multi-million dollar contract, if I didn't have the opportunity to sell knives to complete strangers in their home. I was able to learn and develop a technique that will impress an executive at a boardroom table by learning and practicing the consultative strategies as a representative at Mrs. Jones' kitchen table.

You've learned that the consultative sale builds upon traditional techniques to give you the sales person far greater control in a presentation. As a result, you will be on point. Your proposition will be concise and relevant,. You will be able to identify the customer's needs quickly, align your product with the correct solution, and always add value beyond their expectations.

Consultative selling is about enabling the client to sell themselves.

What used to be an anxiety-producing "close" will become a comfortable suggestion or recommendation that your client will sell to themselves, without any force on your part. You will leave your sales call feeling as though you truly helped your client find a solution to his or her problem. This is better than leaving with an overwhelming feeling of unease, guilt or even failure.

If you aspire to present to senior executives under the lights of the boardroom, just remember that much of what I learned about selling to high powered executives, I learned in the toughest call of all, selling knives at the kitchen table.

## Summary Points

- Identify a customer's true needs and provide a compelling solution to a problem.

- Increased confidence in your presentation will give you an increased closing rate.

- Change up your presentation. Stay off script. Keep it dynamic for yourself and ultimately for your customer.

- Definitely don't script your closing. Be present in the moment, be aware of your audience, be sincere.

- You can't listen to what the customer needs while you are talking.

- Don't try to cover everything and hope something sticks – know when to talk and when to keep quiet.

- Get people talking and comfortable. Ask lots of questions.

- If you know you've set out to help a customer make a good decision, you can feel positive about them buying your product.

- Be on the customer's team. Add value for the customer and you will be valued and receive value in return.

After surviving a near fatal head-on collision with a drunk driver, Hal Elrod became living proof that miracles are possible as he went on to become a National Champion, Hall of Fame business achiever, Life Empowerment Coach, and is one of the top Inspirational and Youth speakers in the world. From Fortune 500 companies like Countrywide and Fidelity to high profile youth organizations including Boys & Girls Club of America, Hal inspires and empowers tens of thousands of people each year to overcome life's adversities so they can Love the Life They Have While Creating the Life of Their Dreams.

# Closing the Gap
## Becoming The Person You Are Destined to Become, Living The Life You've Always Wanted

### Hal Elrod

## The Potential Gap

Selling is, I believe, a microcosm of life. Days filled with a broad array of ups and downs, opportunities and challenges, victories and defeats -- all of which contribute to the growth of the individual.

I once heard Jim Rohn share the following quote which forever changed my way of thinking and ultimately transformed my life.

"Success is something you attract," he said, "...by the person you become."

I can tell you from my own transformative journey, from the depths of mediocrity -- living all areas of my life somewhere in between below average and average -- to a top-producing sales rep, national champion sales manager, international speaker and bestselling author, that Jim's sentiments are still true today, and as true for my own transformation as they will be for yours.

Most salespeople live each day on the wrong side of a huge gap that separates who they are from who they can become. Often frustrated with themselves, their lack of consistent motivation, effort and results (sales, income, etc.), they spend a majority of their time procrastinating and *thinking* a lot about the actions they should be taking to create the results that they want, but then not taking those actions.

Most salespeople know what they need to do, they just don't do what they know.

This "potential" gap varies in size from person to person, but it is absolutely possible and attainable for you to live your life on the right side of your potential gap and become the person that you are destined to become.

Whether you are just starting out in sales and have big goals and high hopes for yourself, or if you have been in the game of selling for a while, but just haven't been able to close that gap and consistently produce at the level you know you are capable of - this chapter will show you how to go from where you are, accepting less than yourself than what you know is possible, to being extraordinary and living the life you've always wanted.

As I share my own story of overcoming my own fears, insecurities and challenges, it is my hope that you will find inspiration in closing the gap for yourself and becoming the person you *know* you can become.

## Moments of Decision

My career in direct sales began unexpectedly just one month after my 19th birthday.

I had just finished my first year of college and was living my dream as a radio disc jockey, going by the hip moniker *'Yo Pal' Hal,* when my college buddy, Teddy Watson, took me with him one day to the Cutco office where he worked in Fresno, California.

At the time I was unaware that Teddy's "routine" stop by the office was really intended to introduce me to his manager, Jesse Levine.

"No thanks, I'm not a salesman," was my response when Jesse offered me a job and a spot in the upcoming three day training program, which took place that weekend. Besides, I was hosting my radio show from midnight to 6 a.m. on Friday and Saturday nights, so I couldn't possibly attend training each day from 9 a.m. to 4 p.m. Right?

Within minutes of explaining the *features and benefits* of the direct sales position with Cutco's distributor, Vector Marketing, Jesse was somehow able to convince me to sign up for training and quite literally forego my sleep that weekend.

On the second day of my training seminar, operating on zero hours of rest, something magical happened that would change my life forever. I made a decision, and as one of my mentors, Anthony Robbins, always says, "It is in our moments of decision that our destiny is shaped."

The decision I made would change the course of my life and me as a person, forever, although I couldn't have known it at the time.

## How Committed Are You?

Jesse explained there was an opportunity for us trainees to win some additional pieces of Cutco to add to our samples through something called the Fast-Start Contest. It took place during our first 10 days selling, and consisted of different sales levels, with prizes that got bigger and better the more you sold.

He then shared with us some exciting news, that the 49-year old Fast-Start record had just been broken the week before, by a young woman just an hour and a half south of us in Bakersfield, who had sold over $12,000 in her first 10 days.

Something inside me flipped like a switch, and I thought to myself, *"If she can do it, so can I."* I could hardly contain the nervous energy I was feeling for my new goal.

Part of my excitement was based on my vision of Jesse's reaction. He was quickly becoming someone I very much admired and I just couldn't wait to see him jumping up and down with joy when he heard my news!

As the last of my fellow trainees left for the day, I approached him.

"Hey Jesse, I have some exciting news to tell you." I could hardly contain myself.

"I want to break the Fast-Start record!"

"Hmm," he said standing there calmly, nodding his head and scratching his fingertips on his chin, processing my exciting news and looking as if he were carefully crafting a mind-blowing response.

Boy, this was going to be good!

"Do you know what that means?" he asked.

"I don't understand," I replied. I was confused.

"What do you mean, 'Do I know what that means'?" I replied.

"Well, I'll be honest with you, Hal...at least one person in every training class tells me that they're going to break the record, but no one has ever done it. I'm asking you if you have any idea what it will take for you to sell over $12,000 to break the record."

My level 10 enthusiasm plummeted to about a level two and Jesse's response to my news was anything but how I had imagined it in my mind.

"I guess it means that I want to break the record and I'm willing to try."

"But see, Hal," he told me.

"Being *willing to try* won't make it happen. Every sales rep that says they want to break the record is *willing to try*, but they're not willing to fully commit to doing the work that it takes to overcome the challenges and rejection and continue giving it everything they have even when they are discouraged and feel like giving up. If you're really committed to breaking the Fast-Start record, I believe you can do it and I can show you how, but I have to know... How committed are you?"

Wow! I had never really been asked that question before in my life about anything. I had never been a member of a team, never excelled in school and never taken a job very seriously. I don't know if I even grasped what it meant to be committed to something.

The next words that came out of my mouth did so without checking with my brain first.

"Jesse, I am one-hundred percent committed."

"What!?" I'm screaming in my head.

Did I have any idea what I was saying or how I was going to follow through on what I was saying? The reality is, I didn't. But I came to realize, much later in my selling career, that when you are committed, the "how" reveals itself.

"Are you sure?" confirmed Jesse.

"You're going to have to work really hard, probably harder than you've ever worked in your life. Are you sure you want to commit to that?"

"Absolutely! I am totally, 100% committed. Just tell me what I need to do and I'll do it."

Although I did not fully grasp what I was getting myself into, in the moment that I committed to the decision I had made to break the Fast-Start record, *"the how"* began to reveal itself. In the next 10 days, my destiny began to take shape.

## Believing In the Belief Others Have In You

Nine days after I made the commitment to Jesse, I was sitting on 56 completed Cutco demonstrations with 37 sales made, for a total of $10,876 - just a little more than $1,300 away from setting the new all-time Fast-Start record.

I can honestly tell you that while I was scared to death that I might not reach my goal, my commitment to give it everything I had until the end kept me going, and I finished my 10th day in miraculous fashion.

I completed six demonstrations and made five sales totaling $4,182 for the day, contributing to my grand total of $15,058 and a new Fast-Start company record!

Everything seemed surreal and I couldn't have imagined life getting any better. I had never experienced such feelings of pride and confidence in myself and confidence in what was possible when I was completely and unconditionally *committed* to a goal and to the process that was necessary to achieve it.

Looking back, I now realize that I didn't fully believe that I could break the record, but Jesse did. He knew it was possible. I was able to persevere through all of my doubts, fears and challenges by drawing strength from his confidence and belief in me. I would have given up long before I reached my goal, had it not been for his unwavering commitment to my success.

That experience taught me that sometimes you have to believe in the belief that others have in you, until your own belief catches up. And never underestimate the impact that your belief in others can have in their lives.

## Rearview Mirror Syndrome

Although I had set the new company Fast-Start record, I had yet to become the person whose thoughts and actions were consistent with attracting the level of success that I wanted and my weekly sales results began to reflect this painful truth.

A lifetime of fears and insecurities, as well as an arsenal of self-destructive habits, behaviors and routines quickly pulled me down from my 15 minutes of fame as the *Fast-Start Record Breaker* back into the comforts of mediocrity, where I felt safe.

I was still living my life on the wrong side of my potential gap, miles away from the person I was destined to become. There I was -- living an average life in a metaphorical mobile home on the side of the grand canyon of my potential, while across the canyon I could see a vision of me creating the life I wanted as a top-producing sales rep, but I couldn't figure out how to close the gap.

> *Most people suffer from the self-limiting dysfunction I call rearview mirror syndrome – they drive through life with their subconscious mind constantly looking in their own self-limiting rear-view mirror. They filter every choice they make…through the limitations of their past experiences.*

If this sounds familiar to you, knowing that you are capable of doing, having and being so much more, but seemingly unable to manifest this elusive reality of "more" that you are destined for, then you are not alone.

Most people suffer from the self-limiting dysfunction I call *rearview mirror syndrome* – they drive through life with their subconscious mind constantly looking in their own self-limiting rear-view mirror. They filter every choice they make, from what time they will wake up in the morning, to which goals they will set, to what they allow themselves to consider is possible, through the limitations of their past experiences.

They want to create a better life, but they don't know how to see it any other way than it has always been.

While it's understandable and at times wise to check your rearview mirror and use your past as a reference point, you must stay present to the reality that who you have been up until this point is not a life-sentence, unless you allow it to be.

You do not have to be limited by your past, and in fact, your future literally exists as *pure possibility*. There are no limits to what you can do with your life this year, the rest of this month, this week, and as soon as you finish reading this chapter -- *today*.

## That Which Doesn't Kill You…

One year and a half after I began selling Cutco, just when I was starting to get the hang of it, life, as I knew it, ended. Driving from a division sales meeting one night, I was hit head on by a drunk driver at over 70 mph, followed by a second car traveling the same speed crashing into my driver's side door.

In one twisted moment of fate, my body was crushed, my leg, arm, pelvis, elbow and eye-socket fractured, my left ear and radial nerve nearly severed and my brain permanently damaged.

I was unable to withstand the unimaginable pain and my mind and body went into a comatose state. Six days later I woke in a hospital bed, attached to life support and given no choice but to face my difficult reality. I had fractured 13 bones, would suffer from permanent brain damage, and the clincher - I might never walk again.

This type of tragedy befalls other people, right? I mean, this doesn't happen to you or I, or the people we love, does it? Even being in my body, broken and stunned, I can remember how difficult my circumstances were to accept. The surreal feelings I experienced after breaking the Fast-Start Record couldn't even be spoken in the same sentence of the magnitude of what I was feeling after my accident, and yet it seemed like only yesterday that I was on top of the world. Now, it had all been taken away from me.

I was faced with another moment of decision, the outcome of which would once again determine my destiny. While I would have never wished for my new circumstances, although I didn't choose them, the reality was that I couldn't change them either. I could, however, choose both an empowering attitude and response in the midst of these challenging circumstances, and that is what I did.

I decided to fully accept all of the circumstances I could not change. I was free from the limitations of living life as a victim and able to focus 100% of my time, energy and efforts on my recovery. I spoke only of creating an exciting and ever-improving future, rather than complain about my plight in life. I decided to focus my attention on all that I had to be grateful for in my life, rather than feel sad about what happened and the many freedoms that had been taken away from me.

Just three weeks after doctors made the grim prognosis that I may never walk again, I took my first step. Four more weeks and I was released from the hospital. Despite doctors' orders, I went back to work selling Cutco, went on to reach my goal of selling over $100,000 that year and finished as the #6 sales rep in the company.

The year that began with me lying in a hospital bed, broken and afraid, ended much differently.

It has been said that what doesn't kill you, makes you stronger. While this may be true, you do not have to personally endure painful events to learn from them. Learning from the trials and tribulations of others, such as the authors of this book, can be the quickest way for you to gain the knowledge you need.

I hope my story serves as evidence for you that there are no valid excuses for not achieving your goals. None. If I can do it, you can do it. To do so though, you must value your goals, dreams and commitments more than you value your excuses.

An effective way to do this is by putting your goals in writing and telling them to every person you know. Doing so will naturally raise the value that you place on them. This happens automatically because the more you look at a goal, and the more you talk about it, the more you feel its importance and the more real it becomes to you.

## A Painfully Enlightening Realization

During the course of my six-year career as a sales rep and manager with Cutco, I felt like I was always chasing success, but never really figuring out how to stay consistently motivated. I could get fired up for short bursts, pump out a good sales week, but then it was back into my same old bad habits of procrastination and daily routines that were less than productive.

What I failed to realize was that it was me who needed to change, to transform, in order to consistently achieve the success I knew I was capable of.

In the fall of 2004, at age 25, I was inducted into the Cutco/Vector Hall of Fame.

Just when I had achieved what I thought was the pinnacle of success and was ready to retire from selling to write my first book and pursue my other passions, I experienced what I like to call a "painfully enlightening realization."

The night of my Hall of Fame induction ceremony was overwhelming for me. Surrounded by my family, friends and colleagues, I felt a myriad of intense emotions - from deep gratitude and appreciation, to a sense of personal pride and overall relief. Little did I know that this was about to be a new beginning that would forever transform my life and ultimately, the lives of many other salespeople.

The morning after, the annual awards ceremony began, and the top sellers—two reps that had sold over $200,000 of Cutco for the year—were awarded a pristine Rolex watch.

Something inside me snapped!

It wasn't the watch that got my attention, it was the painful realization that these sales reps were being rewarded for something that I had failed to do. I felt like a phony. The night before I had accepted my Hall of Fame trophy with a sense of pride that now felt undeniably inauthentic.

Never in my Cutco career had I worked consistently over the course of an entire year, never had I given it my all, and now it was painfully apparent that I was *still* living on the wrong side of the grand canyon of my potential.

But how could I close gap?

All I knew for sure was that I would never be able to look at my Hall of Fame trophy without feeling like a complete fraud unless I did something about it. So, I made a new decision, one that came as an absolute surprise to me—I decided to commit to one more year selling Cutco.

Feeling excited (with the fear to set in later) about these newfound possibilities, I opened up my laptop at the conference and typed "My Commitments for 2005". This is what I wrote:

- I will double my best year and sell over 200k of Cutco.

- I will pay it forward and also lead 10 of my peers to sell 200k.

- I will write and publish my first book, *Taking Life Head On!: The Hal Elrod Story)*

These goals seemed more like fantasies to me, and I had no idea *how* I was going to accomplish any of them. I did, however, have one thing going for me, something Jesse taught me about six years before... I was committed.

## The Transformation Process
## Step One: Learning From Those Who Have Done It

One of the first things I did was call every sales rep I knew who had sold over $200,000 of Cutco in one year. I wanted to know *specifically* how they did it.

Even though I was nervous to call some of these top producers, I overcame my fear and made calls to Cutco's elite: *Adam Curchack, Brad Weimert, Jeremy Reisig, John Ruhlin, Bret Barrie, Tanya Strohmaier* and *Jon Berghoff.* This group made up the select few that had somehow been able to figure out the elusive formula for consistently producing extraordinary results.

When I called them, I had a list of written questions, addressing both the mental/emotional aspects of achieving such a big goal, as well as the logistics of precisely what they did from day-to-day, and week-to-week, to make it happen.

I asked, "What motivated you to go for 200k?" "How did you stay motivated?" "Were you ever scared you might fail?" "How did you deal with that fear?" "What specifically was your daily/weekly schedule like?" "How many phone calls did you make and when?" "How many appointments did you do and when?" "What were your biggest challenges?" "What were the biggest keys to your success?"

> *Successful people make a habit of consistently doing what unsuccessful people only do some of the time.*

Once I had "interviewed" each person, I began to see that they weren't that different than me, and now I had a big picture perspective informing me which types of consistent behaviors, actions, habits and routines would be required for me to reach my goal.

It was no coincidence that most of these were things I was accustomed to doing, just not consistently. The quote I had heard many times, *"Successful people make a habit of consistently doing what unsuccessful people only do some of the time,"* was starting to make a lot of sense.

So, I learned I had to act consistently, but I still wasn't sure what I was supposed to be doing. Figuring that out was my next step.

## Step Two: Defining & Committing To The Process

Every result is created by a process, consisting of specific actions, necessary to producing that result.

By figuring out specifically which actions you or someone else have taken in the past to create a sales result, you can make the necessary increases/adjustments to your process to increase your results. Once I learned what others had done to sell 200k, I had a foundation to work from and just needed to tweak the numbers a little bit to define my own process.

I went through my schedule from the year before and added up the following:

1. How many phone calls I made.
2. How many appointments I scheduled.
3. How many appointments I completed.
4. How many sales I made.
5. How much I sold.

By knowing my numbers from the year before, I knew roughly how many phone calls and appointments I needed to complete in order to sell 200k. Now, I had a process to commit to.

I determined that in order to sell over $200,000 of Cutco for the year, all I had to do was consistently make an average of 100 calls every week in order to schedule an average 12 appointments, which would result in an average 10 sales for approximately $4,000 per week.

The trick was going to be staying committed to the process, without being emotionally attached to my results. I kept a big picture perspective - there was no reason to get emotionally distraught when things weren't going as planned.

Bottom line - as long as I stayed committed to the process of making 100 calls per week, the law of averages would work itself out and I would reach or exceed my goal.

But here's the thing – how would I stay committed to the process for an entire year, when I never had before?

## Step Three: Planning A Weekly Schedule And Routine

Once I knew which actions I had to take and what the process would be to reach my goal, then I had to plan them into my daily and weekly schedule. No longer could I be content waking up each morning without a plan for the day.

I needed to be intentional and purposeful regarding what I did with my time. If I were going to take it to the next level, I would need to become a planner and I would need to establish consistency in my daily and weekly routines.

That was something that each of the elite Cutco reps shared with me during our phone call. Each of them followed a consistent weekly schedule that included time planned every week, usually an hour on Sundays, to review the previous week and plan their upcoming weekly schedule.

For the most part, they woke up the same time each morning, made their phone calls during the same times each day, scheduled their appointments for the same days each week and took the same day or two off for rest and rejuvenation.

Most of them also had time blocks scheduled each week to work on non-work activities, such as cleaning the house or running errands. By scheduling their non-work activities in advance, they ensured that those activities weren't available to distract them or to use as an excuse not to do the most important work-related activities.

So since almost all successful salespeople seem to plan and follow successful daily and weekly routines, consisting of their most important, income-producing activities, I decided I'd better do the same. Sitting down to plan my schedule for the week was challenging in itself at first, since I hadn't yet created a habit of doing it, but it was my rearview mirror syndrome that left me wondering... "How could I get myself to follow through with the schedule and routines that I planned?"

## Step Four: Initiating A System For Accountability

Little happens in this world without some form of accountability.

Accountability is the act of being responsible to somebody else or to others or responsible for some action or result. Accountability can exist in various forms, such as a deadline or due date, a negative consequence or a potential reward.

You have been leveraging the power of accountability to produce results since you were a child, unless you were one of those weird kids in school that did your homework on the day it was assigned and read textbooks for fun. As for the rest of us, we turned in our homework, studied for tests, and even showed up to school all because of the system of accountability initiated by our parents and teachers.

Now that we're all grown up and striving to succeed as professional salespeople, we must take responsibility for initiating our own system for accountability. There is more than one option when it comes to choosing an Accountability Source for your Accountability System. Some examples are:

**Team up with an Accountability Partner.** This could be another salesperson in your office, or even someone in a different industry. The important thing is that you are both working towards similar types of goals, so that you can understand and relate to which actions each other needs to be taking.

**Find a dedicated Mentor.** This could be your Sales Manager, a leader in your office or a seasoned sales professional with proven results in another industry. What is important is that they are willing and agree to provide you with the dedicated one-on-one time you need, keeping track of your commitments each week and checking in with you to see that you followed through.

**Assemble an Accountability Team.** This is the route I took in 2005, assembling approximately 20 sales reps from different parts of the country and facilitating a conference call each week to check in on everyone's commitments, such as phone calls, appointments and sales. As the leader of my team, I felt responsible for walking my talk, setting the right example and being 100% accountable to following through with my commitments. There were many mornings when I didn't want to get out of bed and make the phone calls I had committed to, but knowing I would have to admit that to my Accountability Team was always enough leverage for me to get up and make it happen.

**Hire a Professional Coach.** Hiring a Professional Coach (PC) has been one of the best investments I have ever taken a chance on, and becoming a PC is one of the most rewarding decisions I have ever made. I say that because my income almost doubled the first year I hired a PC, while virtually every other area of my life improved. This was largely due to my PC being trained in how to professionally hold salespeople accountable, as well as the fact that, I paid him a significant amount of money to do just that, which causes me to take my commitments very seriously.

Accountability is the most important and yet most often missing piece of The Transformation Process. Even if you get through the first three steps—Learning From Those That Have Done It, Defining & Committing To The Process, and Planning A Daily & Weekly Routine - but you don't have an effective Accountability System, you are likely to get stuck looking and living into your rearview mirror, falling back into your old behaviors, habits and routines.

## The Transformation Process Works

Despite all of my doubts and fears related to being able to breakthrough my limitations to achieve my goals, I did it.

Using The Transformation Process, I was able to close the gap on my potential to become the better version of myself. This enabled me to reach all of my personal goals for the year—selling over $205,000 of Cutco while writing and publishing my bestselling book, *Taking Life Head On!*

And my goal to pay it forward by leading 10 reps to sell 200k? Well, I led conference calls every Sunday and offered support through daily emails and telephone calls and although 10 reps didn't reach the goal, six of us sold 200k in 2005 - the most reps to surpass that mark in company history.

It took almost six months for my internal, mental and emotional transformation to catch up with the transformation in my behaviors and routines. I still saw myself through my old rearview mirror, which reflected my past laziness, lack of motivation and consistency.

Then one day in May, one of my colleagues pointed out how different I had become. He said that he was impressed by how focused I was on working everyday towards my goals and that I didn't allow things to distract me - things like watching television, staying out late or making excuses.

"Really? I'm different...?" I asked myself.

The more I thought about it, the more I saw that I had changed because my actions and behaviors had changed.

It worked for me, but would this process work for others as well?

> *The Transformation Process*
> *1. Learn From Those Who Have Done It.*
> *2. Define & Commit To The Process.*
> *3. Plan A Weekly Schedule & Routine.*
> *4. Initiate A System For Accountability.*

## Begin Your Transformation Today

After retiring from Cutco in 2005, I co-founded Global Empowerment Coaching with my good friend and business partner, Jon Berghoff. We provide life, sales, business and leadership coaching. We have worked with hundreds of salespeople, managers, executives and business owners to help them become the person they need to be to create the life they have always wanted.

Leading our clients through *The Transformation Process,* I have seen them consistently produce extraordinary results - from significant increases in sales and income to more fulfillment and balance with life and work; it happens again and again with virtually every person we work with. I have seen them overcome their self-imposed limitations and take on goals - goals that they once considered outside the realm of what was possible for themselves - with a newfound sense of confidence and motivation.

These results are not of luck, nor are they reserved for the chosen few - transformation is available for everyone. You can become the person you've always known you are capable of being, the successful person who will consistently attract success into your life and you need not wait another second… your transformation can begin today.

## Summary Points

- Success is something you attract by the person you become.

- You might be committed to trying, but are you fully committed to doing the work and overcoming challenges and rejection? What will you do when it's hard and you feel like giving up?

- When you are fully committed to a goal, the "how" you will achieve it will be revealed to you.

- Most people have Rearview Mirror Syndrome, that is, they drive through life looking back at their self-limiting past and let it define them in the present.

- Ask successful people how they achieved their goals, then do what they did.

- Be intentional and purposeful with time – plan incremental goals, keep a weekly schedule, monitor your progress.

- Be accountable – use deadlines, other people, rewards or demerits, whatever works, to keep you on track and moving toward success.

- Know that change only comes from inside yourself. You are the only one who can make it happen!

# Charity Information

The authors in this book have dedicated their time and talents so that their charities could be the recipients of their royalties from this project. By buying this book, you've contributed to the author's favorite and worthwhile charities.

The charities and their author/benefactors are listed here:

## Jeffrey Gitomer: Thompson Child & Family Focus
www.thompsoncff.org

Thompson Child & Family Focus was originally created in the late 1800's to serve North Carolina's orphans. Today, dedicated staff pour love and expertise into caring for children and families that society treats as invisible. Each year, over 300 children benefit from Thompson's continuum of care. Their top priorities are to give young people and their parents the necessary tools to ensure stability and, when possible, to keep families together.

## Jon Berghoff & Jon Vroman: Front Row Foundation
www.frontrowfoundation.org

Front Row Foundation helps people who are braving critical health challenges live their lives to the fullest. The organization puts people in front row seats at the event of their dreams, so they can fully embrace the healing powers of music, sports, laughter or any positive experience to fuel their desire for life.

## Carl Drew: Life Climb

www.lifeclimb.org

LifeClimb delivers adventure in the classroom and wilderness to help teens climb towards a better life. The organization helps teens understand they are in charge of their decisions and that their decisions create their future outdoor adventures, seminars and expeditions. These experiences empower teens with the tools and resources they need to ignite their passion for life and overcome the challenges they face daily.

## John Ruhlin: Campus Crusade

www.ccci.org

The Campus Crusade for Christ International helps bring people to faith in Jesus Christ with an emphasis on evangelism and discipleship.

## Brad Britton: MIQLAT

www.miqlat.org

MIQLAT mobilizes people to help children and families living in conditions of poverty, despair and violence. The organization provides programs assisting the improvement of communities and specifically young potential leaders. We minister to the physical, emotional and spiritual needs of the community, also rendering aid in times of crisis. MIQLAT is a Hebrew word that means "a place of refuge and hope."

## Dan Casetta: Alzheimer's Foundation of America

www.alzfdn.org

The Alzheimer's Foundation provides optimal care and services to individuals confronting dementia, and to their caregivers and families—through member organizations dedicated to improving quality of life.

## John Edwin: World Vision

www.worldvision.org

World Vision is a Christian humanitarian organization dedicated to working with children, families and their communities worldwide to reach their full potential by tackling the causes of poverty and injustice. The organization serves close to 100 million people in nearly 100 countries around the world.

## Jason Scheckner: ASPCA

www.aspca.org

The ASPCA was founded in 1866 to alleviate the injustices animals faced then and they continue to battle cruelty today. Whether it's saving a pet that has been accidentally poisoned, fighting to pass humane laws, rescuing animals from abuse or sharing resources with shelters across the country, they work toward the day in which no animal will live in pain or fear.

## Paulette Tucciarone: Doctors Without Borders

www.doctorswithoutborders.org

Doctors Without Borders or Médecins Sans Frontières is an international medical humanitarian organization working in more than 60 countries to assist people whose survival is threatened by violence, neglect or catastrophe. These conditions are often due to armed conflict, epidemics, malnutrition, exclusion from healthcare and natural disasters. The organization often speaks out to bring attention to neglected crises, to challenge inadequacies and abuse of the aid system and to advocate for improved medical treatments and protocols.

## Hal Elrod: MADD

www.madd.org

MADD or Mothers Against Drunk Driving is committed to supporting victims who have been hurt by individuals driving under the influence of alcohol or drugs, to aid the families of these victims and to increase public awareness of the problem of drinking and drugged driving.

## Ranjeet Pawar: Industrial Technical Center Mhila

www.ranjeetpawar.com/school.html

The all girls' school, Industrial Technical Center Mhila, is located in the village of Ailum, approximately 60 miles north of New Delhi. The school provides young women from neighboring villages the opportunity to continue their education beyond the 6th grade level. Students are taught various technical trades at little or no cost to themselves. The young women graduate with a stronger sense of empowerment and a greater understanding of their future value as entrepreneurs.

## Fi Mazanke: The Brite Foundation

The BRITE Foundation stands for "Bridges Reading Inspires Individuals to Excel." The organization, established by a group of inspired mothers, is committed to building and expanding the library at Bridges Academy in St. Charles, Illinois. The Brite Foundation has already raised funds to purchase 5,000 books for the library.

## Jerry Liu: The LIU Institute of Child Development

The LIU Foundation is a non-profit organization that offers grants for parents of autistic children in China. Because of the limited understanding of autism in China, governmental support on special education in the public system is deficient. The LIU Foundation provides extra financial support as well as resources for parents who are looking to receive extra training or schooling for their autistic children.

## Adam Stock: Smile Train
www.smiletrain.org

Since March of 2000, the Smile Train has provided free cleft surgery to nearly 320,000 children. It's easy to love a charitable organization whose mission results in helping thousands of children smile all over the world. 100% of all donations to Smile Train are used for programs, not overhead costs.

## John Israel:
## The Michael J. Fox Foundation for Parkinson's Research
www.michaeljfox.org

The Michael J. Fox Foundation is dedicated to finding a cure for Parkinson's disease within the decade through an aggressively funded research agenda and to ensuring the development of improved therapies for those living with Parkinson's today.

# Acknowledgements

At the end of the film *Into the Wild*, a true story about Chris McCandless and his adventure to find truth, the words "Happiness is only real when shared." are revealed as the final answer to his quest. *Cutting Edge Sales*, in so many ways, was a shared experience. It was built to spread its influence through the causes it will support and the lessons it will teach, yet only happened because of so many whose support will send ripples that they may never see.

To my dad, **Chuck**, for teaching me to learn something from everything and my mom, **Sue**, for always saying yes, and letting me explore the world. I thank you both for every morsel of life that I experience. To **Bill** and **Mike**, for being the best older brothers I could wish for and for teaching me life's hard lessons - without inflicting too much pain.

To **Vector Marketing** and **Cutco Cutlery**. Your commitment to products, people and programs that allow young people to succeed is rare, life changing and forever in my heart. To **Randy Gilbert**, **Kim Foster** and **Morgan James Publishing** for believing in, supporting and massaging this book to the finish line. Your trust, hard work and service will give back to the world, one page at a time.

To all our authors for believing in this project and meeting the most demanding of deadlines. Because of your care and effort, others can learn from your wisdom and benefit from your gifts.

To **Jeffrey Gitomer** for your excellence, your time and your influence on this project. You are not only hilarious, you are brilliant and you deserve all the success that has come your way.

To **Dan Casetta** for your guidance, your influence on my career and your continued example of excellence for the world. A day does not go by that I don't credit you for lessons you taught me.

To **Carl Drew** for inspiring all of us to live our dreams. You think big, you live big and you give even bigger.

To **Brad Britton** for sending me exactly the right notes at exactly the right time during my sales career. Your trust, willingness to risk and simplicity are all models for us to follow.

To **John Ruhlin** for being the greatest salesperson I have ever met and for teaching me to sell by giving to others. Your trust in this book has served it more than words can describe.

To **Jon Vroman** for living life in the Front Row. Your work continuously creates magical moments that will send ripples far beyond what we will ever see.

To **Fi Mazenkie** for teaching us to look inward for answers. Your presence, your insight and your light are shining on this project.

To **Ranjeet Pawar** for being the consummate leader and a passionate entrepreneur. Your story and your perspective will transform every reader of this book.

To **Jerry Liu** for your ability to teach us what creates champions. Your integrity as a person serves as an example for us all.

To **John Edwin** for making our world a healthier community, from the inside out. You are full of love John and it shows in everything you do.

To **Paulette Tucciarone** for unparalleled real world experience and a deep understanding of people. Both of which make this book special and our country fortunate for your service.

To **John Israel** for choosing to be a leader of leaders. It has been an honor to witness your growth, and see the legacy you are going to leave.

To **Adam Stock** for reminding us that in order to serve in our businesses, we have to keep sight on what matters. Your lessons will grow the bottom line.

To **Jason Scheckner** for your leadership and your ability to articulate for others how to succeed. Your obvious gifts as a teacher will keep giving.

To **Hal Elrod** for encouraging us all to enjoy the life we have while creating the life of our dreams. There are very few people who can claim selflessness and you are one of them.

To **Karl Gedris** for telling me about a goofy job selling knives. With all that we have shared, your friendship has meant the most.

To my greatest inspiration, my teacher, my soul mate and my wife, **Mara**. Your love is pure, authentic and seemingly endless. Thank you. Thank you. Thank you.

# Recommended Books From the Authors

| | |
|---|---|
| Little Red Book of Selling | Jeffrey Gitomer |
| Masters of Sales | Dr. Ivan Misner |
| Influence | Dr. Robert Cialdini |
| No B.S. Sales Success | Dan Kennedy |
| How To Master The Art of Selling | Tom Hopkins |
| The Psychology of Selling (Audio Series) | Brian Tracy |
| Leading an Inspired Life | Jim Rohn |
| Awaken The Giant Within | Anthony Robbins |
| High Trust Selling | Todd Duncan |
| Secrets of The Millionaire Mind | T. Harv Eker |
| The Ultimate Sales Machine | Chet Holmes |
| Psycho-Cybernetics | Maxwell Maltz |
| Think and Grow Rich | Napoleon Hill |
| The Science of Getting Rich | Wallace Wattles |
| Taking Life Head On | Hal Elrod |
| Selling 101 | Zig Ziglar |
| The Attractor Factor | Joe Vitale |
| Relationship Networking | Sandra Yancey |
| All Marketers Are Liars | Seth Godin |

# About Jon Berghoff

**Jon Berghoff**
**Influence Strategist**

Jon began earning a six figure income his first year in business, while still in high school, as a distributor for Cutco Cutlery. Jon compiled a list of records which placed him number one in sales – ultimately achieving what over 1,000,000 other distributors in the 58 year company history had not.

Jon went on to parallel his success managing sales in the health club and wellness industry, once again building a client base of 2,000 plus customers, and a championship sales team from scratch, all by the age of 23.

For more than a decade now, Jon has uncovered, tested and taught sales and influence strategies. Jon's interactive trainings have now reached over 75,000 live students internationally and he has conducted over 3,500 private coaching calls with clients from more than 100 professions and trades.

Jon also blends into his trainings his experience as an endurance athlete - at times running 50, 100, or more miles consecutively, often through extreme conditions. He is a passionate supporter of The Front Row Foundation, a cause which remains close to his heart. Jon recently married the love of his life, Mara Berghoff, on top of Half Dome in Yosemite, CA.

Keep performing at The Cutting Edge by following Jon on
www.geconnection.com/blog

Jon Berghoff is Available

<u>Keynote Speaking - Coaching -</u>
<u>Interactive Training Seminars - Consulting</u>

In the following areas (but not limited to):

**Sales and Marketing Mastery**
**High Level Presentation, Training and Speaking Skills**
**Sales Management and Leadership Training**
**Behavioral Science and Human Achievement**
**Influence Mastery with Self & Others**

Speaking or Training Inquiries: speaking@geconnection.com
General Information & Free Email Newsletter:
www.geconnection.com
Blog: www.geconnection.com/blog

# CUTTING EDGE SALES
## 3 FREE BONUS GIFTS

**CLAIM YOUR FREE BONUS GIFTS RIGHT NOW – A $197 VALUE!**

## FREE GIFT#1 EXCLUSIVE AUTHOR INTERVIEWS

How would you like to be handed exclusive, up-close access to our authors? This is a special opportunity to gain **brand new secrets** directly from the *Cutting Edge Sales* authors. Delivered in quick, easy-to-absorb audio interviews, Jon Berghoff extracts insights and wisdom that go behind the scenes of *Cutting Edge Sales*.

You will discover philosophies, sales tips, influence strategies, business-building insights, inspiration and information that will **elevate your sales business to the next level** – immediately.

## FREE GIFT#2 SELLING THE INVISIBLE E-COURSE

Are you ready to master the skills of influence? This is a condensed audio and workbook E-Course version of **Selling The Invisible - Winning The Sales Game Through Mastering Influence,** the bestselling program from Jon Berghoff's WINFLUENCE Training Series. Selling The Invisible gives you a glimpse into the playbook of the world's top performing sales professionals.

In this 7 part E-Course, you will discover:

*A simple understanding of influence that will **transform your business** from the inside out.

*3 Principles of Peak Performers with **step-by-step tools** to implement them TODAY.

*How to **master the prospecting game** – once and for all.

*Jon's proven method for designing **"the perfect sales presentation"** – every time.

*4 Influence Triggers that reveal how people buy, and **how to outsell your competition**.

\*Jon's personal success principles that tens of thousands of students, and Fortune 500 companies have leveraged to **championship sales success.**

# FREE GIFT#3 52 WEEK *CUTTING EDGE SALES* EXECUTION TRAINING

Are you ready to take action? Would you like us to make it easy for you along the way? Each week, for 52 weeks, we will deliver directly to your inbox, a short lesson pulled from *Cutting Edge Sales*. These lessons will be packaged to quickly and easily apply to your business, your sales and your ability to reach your goals. This is the **smartest**, most **effective** way to maximize what *Cutting Edge Sales* has to offer!

## Go NOW to:
## www.cuttingedgesalesbook.com/bonusgifts